It is said that before entering the sea
a river trembles with fear.

She looks back at the path she has traveled,
from the peaks of the mountains,
the long winding road crossing forests and villages.

And in front of her,
she sees an ocean so vast,
that to enter there seems nothing more
than to disappear forever.

But there is no other way.
The river cannot go back.
Nobody can go back.
To go back is impossible in existence.

The river needs to take the risk
of entering the ocean
because only then will fear disappear,
because that's where the river will know
it's not about disappearing into the ocean,
but of becoming the ocean

"The River"
– Attributed to Gibran Kahlil Gibran

fade in

Scene 1

Everything is white.

The distant beeping sounds of a machine can be heard.

(Male voice over)

Those who had a near-death experience say that they went into a long white tunnel before coming back to life... Does anyone know what's at the end of the tunnel? Do we really make our own choices or is someone pulling the strings?

When Earth, and everything on it, is just a speck of dust in this universe, can you imagine how much string all those lives need? *Long whistle*

Whether we are born in New York or Kandahar, rich or poor, with X or Y chromosomes, with Down syndrome or not, single or married. Oops! No, that last one we bring onto ourselves.
In the beginning, there was Adam and Eve. Then it became Adam and Adam, Eve and Eve... But to be fair, all of us have made such a mess of our relationships that we are really at a loss of what to do with ourselves.

Enough! I'm over-analyzing again.
It's too much to think about.
It is said that a single man lives like a king but dies like a dog, and that a married man lives like a dog but dies like a king. In the end, it doesn't matter, we're all going to die.
So, I choose to live like a king!

But when I die, where will I go? To hell? No, definitely not, I'm allergic to the heat.

To heaven? Not sure I deserve it...
The apple has always been my favorite fruit even though I have a flawless criminal record...

William (52 years old) is being pulled out of an MRI machine, engulfed in white light.

Suddenly a small, cheeky smile lights up his face.

Okay, I'll go where the pretty women are.

Abboudy Mallah

The Puppeteer

KAPH

The following text has been modified from its original version. Written as a movie script, it has been formatted to fit this book.

CHARACTERS

William
52 years old
Successful businessman

Sofia
32 years old
Interior designer
Jack's wife

Jack
35 years old
Physiotherapist
Sofia's husband

Rabih
35 years old
Gynecologist
Jack's friend

Nady
35 years old
Entrepreneur
Jack's friend

Jihane
60 years old
Sofia's mother

Rajin
Jihane's building concierge

Tony
William's business partner

Jamal
Board member at William's company

Selim
Board member at William's company

Dr. Omar
Founder of
the Children's Cancer Center
William's friend

Dr. Fouad
50 years old
William's doctor
and friend

Mateo
30 years old
William's nurse

Miuca
32 years old
Artist
William's love interest

Nabil
45 years old
Head of the Physiotherapy Department
Jack's boss

Solange
45 years old
Sexy woman at the Night Club

Scene 2
Jack and Sofia's house at night

Soft music fills the air. Candles are lit in the bedroom and rose petals are on the floor. Sophia (32 years old), dressed in sexy lingerie, holding a champagne flute in her hand, sits on the edge of the bathtub checking the temperature of the water in the bubble bath adorned with floating rose petals.

On a small table, a bottle of champagne sits in an ice bucket near an empty flute and a platter of cheese. Next to the refreshments, a handwritten note says "Happy 2nd Wedding Anniversary my love."

Scene 3
Hospital entrance at night

Jack (35 years old) rushes out of the hospital carrying his briefcase and gets into Rabih's 4×4 Jeep.

Rabih
Why are you so late, man? It's like you're the only physiotherapist in Beirut!

Rabih (35 years old) drives off while Jack is sending a WhatsApp text from his mobile

Scene 4
Jack and Sofia's house

Sophia is lighting some incense and enjoying the smell. She receives a WhatsApp message on her mobile, checks it, then puts her mobile down. She pauses for a moment before blowing out the candles in front of her.

Cut to

Scene 5
Fishing boat at night

Jack, Rabih and Nady (35 years old) have set up their fishing rods. The boat is anchored in the middle of the sea. They are sitting back, drinking beer and chatting.

Jack
Like it or not, habibi[1] the French have dominated football since 2000. In the last seven world cups, they reached the finals four times, won two of them and lost the other two in penalty kicks...So not even a real loss.

Nady
You and your Frenchie "blondies" team.
You should raise the Zaire flag!

Nady moves over to the cooler. He throws a beer to Rabih and one to Jack. Jack gives Rabih a "listen to this" kind of look.

Jack
Please, explain to that illiterate that it's Congo now. All teams are like that nowadays. Look at your German team, they are not all Aryans you know! Khdeyra, Ozil and Khan! These guys were born and raised in Europe. Can you please open your racist mind a bit?

Nady
I'm gonna open something else...

Jack
Stop talking nonsense and hand me my phone.

Nady takes a phone from a box next to the captain's seat where everyone's phones are placed, and throws it to Jack. Jack trips slightly before catching it.

Jack
I've told you a hundred times not to throw the phone like that! What if it falls in the water?!

Nady
Stick it in some rice, it'll remove the moisture.

Nady stands at the other end of the boat. He starts to pee into the sea.

Rabih
Oh for God's sake!!!

1 Means "darling" in casual Arabic.

Nady
I need to empty so I can refill. Empty, full, empty, full!

Rabih
Go to the other side at least!

Nady
It's too far.

Jack looks at his phone surprised. Strangely, Sophia saw his WhatsApp messages but still hasn't replied.

Rabih
What's the matter?

Jack
Sophia isn't answering any of my messages.

Nady
Lucky you, I wish my wife would do the same.

Rabih
How's it going between you two these days?

Jack
It's shit.

Rabih laughs.

Jack
You know quicksand? That's us, but instead of quick "sand" it's quick "shit."

Rabih
You ain't seen nothing yet. Wait until you have a baby.

Nady finishes peeing, comes back and pinches Jack's cheek. Nady smiles teasingly.

Nady
You want to spread your seed, little one?

Jack moves Nady's hand away from his cheek.

Jack
Don't touch my face! Disgusting!

Rabih
Don't forget this Saturday, it's my son Timi's birthday.

Jack
Sorry man, on Saturdays I go to my doctorate classes. Wait, wasn't Timi born on the twenty-eighth?

Rabih
And Saturday is the twenty-eighth.

Jack is quiet for a moment before realizing something...

Jack
Saturday is the twenty-eighth...so tomorrow is the twenty-seventh...which makes today the twenty-sixth?!!

Jack looks like he has just seen a ghost. He smacks his hand on his forehead and starts running around the boat, gathering the fishing rods.

Jack
Today is the twenty-sixth!!

Rabih
What's the matter??

Nady
Obviously, he doesn't like the twenty-sixth.

Suddenly, Jack stands on the edge of the boat.

Jack
Today is my wedding anniversary!! The twenty-sixth!!

Rabih
Oops! Okay, okay, take it easy!

In a moment of despair, Jack lets himself fall back off the boat into the sea. Rabih and Nady rush to the side of the boat, looking for him.

Scene 6

Jack and Sofia's house

The front door opens. Still wet, Jack comes in and places his belongings on the table. The clock hanging on the wall shows that it's 1 a.m. The dining room table,s is set up for a romantic dinner for two. He enters the bedroom which is pitch black.

At first, Jack doesn't turn on the light, thinking Sophia might be asleep. He enters the bathroom quietly and when he turns on the light, he sees the rose petals, candles and the tub full of water. He goes to the bed and notices that Sophia isn't in it.

Turning on the bedroom light, he sees the rose petals all over the floor and the bed. His eyes move to the closet. Its door is open and there is nothing inside.

He checks Sophia's vanity which is completely empty as well.

It's confirmed: Sophia has left home. Jack lets out a long sigh, closing his eyes in despair. He falls on the bed and just lays there for a moment, staring at the ceiling.

Finally, he picks up his phone and dials Sophia's number.

Telephone Operator
The number you have dialed is currently unavailable. Please try again later.

He throws his phone on the bed while lying there.

Scene 7

William's house

William is doing his morning laps in his pool, outside. Inside his luxurious mansion, Sophia is working in his exquisitely decorated living room. She takes measurements and jots them down in her notebook. The housekeeper gives her a hand.

When William is done with his laps, he climbs out of the pool, puts on his bathrobe, and enters the living room.

William
Bonjour, I'm William.

Sophia
I'm Sophia, from the offices of Bekhazi and Bekhazi.

William
I'm sorry but I have to leave soon and cut our meeting short. Let me brief you quickly and then you can go back to your measurements.

Sophia
Of course.

William
Let's have coffee outside.

On the terrace, they sip their coffee. On the breakfast bar near them lies a full bowl of apples, a few croissants, fruit salad and orange juice.

William
The bookshelf area is the most important. It needs to be emphasized. I also want the wine coolers to be built in on the wall facing it.
In brief, the entire design concept should revolve around these two areas.

Sophia takes notes.

Sophia
I noticed there is no TV. Would you like me to add one in?

William
Definitely not. I'm not that well-off.

Sophia smiles.

William
I'm short on patience. When can I see a draft?

Sophia
Next week?

William
Tomorrow night.

William glances at her hands and notes that she is not wearing an engagement or a wedding ring.

William
The Avalon at 8:30 p.m. No need for the complete plan, a couple of sketches should be fine.

He stands up.

William
I need to be excused, but please go ahead and continue your breakfast.

He leaves before Sophia gets a chance to realize what William has just inflicted on her.

Scene 8

Jack's private clinic

Jack tries calling Sophia again. No answer.
He gets up from his chair and heads toward the reception area where his assistant is working on some files.

Jack
May I use your phone to make a phone call?

His assistant looks surprised.

Assistant
Sure

Jack
I need to call someone who owes me money.
It's unbelievable how people are these days!

He takes her phone and goes into his office.

Scene 9

Interior design office

Sophia is working on William's design plans. Her phone rings. It's an unfamiliar number.

Sophia
Allo?

Jack
Sophia

Sophia
Who is this?

Jack
Jack

Sophia hangs up and gets back to work. Jack calls back, but Sophia's phone is on silent mode. The meeting with her boss, Mr. Bekhazi, is soon. She walks to his office and sits in front of his desk.

Sophia
Mr. Bekhazi, I'm not ready for tonight!

Mr. Bekhazi
But I asked the team to help you with the sketches!
What happened?

Sophia
The sketches are ready. As for the dinner...
I was thinking....

Mr. Bekhazi
Sophia, William is a generous client.

A bit pushy, but he pays in cash! And you know what that's worth these days? That means he's a legend. A god! An extinct species. So, get yourself all dolled up for tonight and be at the Avalon at exactly one minute to 8:30 p.m. Chew your food with a big smile on your face. Have you ever tried chewing with a smile?!

Scene 10

Jihane's house at night

Sophia's mother, Jihane, is watching TV in the dimly lit living room while Sophia is getting ready in her bedroom for her dinner appointment with William.

Jack pulls his car up to Jihane's building. The garage attendant, Rajin, recognizes Jack and lets him through.

Sophia comes out of her room and silently watches Jihane sitting there alone. Jihane feels her stare and turns in surprise that Sophia is dressed up.

Sophia
Bye, Mom.

Jihane
Isn't it too soon for you to start going out?

Sophia
It's work, Mama, I have to go. Bye.

Jack is in the lobby waiting for the elevator. The doors open and Sophia steps out. They are both surprised.

Jack
Hah!

Sophia
What do you want?!

Jack
Nothing, everything is great!

Sophia
Good. Thank God for that.

She walks past him and he grabs her by the elbow.

Jack
Sophia!

Sophia
I really don't have the time for this, Jack,
I have to get to work!

Jack
Work at this time of night?? Splendid!

Sophia
I'm not kidding. I'm in a hurry. If you have something to say, say it quickly.

Jack
I'm sorry. I did forget our wedding anniversary.
You have every right to be upset.
But is that a reason for you to leave the house?!
Aren't you overreacting a bit?

Sophia
Don't you dare belittle me like you always do!
Our problems are much deeper and go way beyond this issue and you know it.
This was the cherry on top.

Jack
Sophia, what did you expect? Look around you.
Do you know any couples who don't have problems?
Ask your girlfriends.

Sophia
Look, I'm really not in the mood to listen to that broken record again. I'm not like other women. Plus, I don't have children to sacrifice or keep my mouth shut for.
And, honestly, I had a really good life before I met you.

Jack
Did you tell your mother?

Sophia
Of course, I did. Better than let her think we are living in honeymoon bliss when this year you've slept more on the sofa than next to me!

Jack
Yeah, well, the sofa doesn't nag!

Sophia gets really mad. She raises her handbag in an attempt to strike him with it, only to hesitate.

Jack
Sorry, sorry. I swear I didn't mean that! I apologize.

Sophia tries to calm herself down.

Sophia
Listen, Jack, let's just take a break to think about what we truly want from this marriage. Maybe... most probably...we're not meant for each other.

Jack
I didn't marry to get divorced!!

Sophia
Well, that's great! But I hope you have a better reason for us to be together.

She pats him on the shoulder and takes off.

Jack
Sophia. Sophia!

Sophia walks toward her car in the parking lot. Jack follows her and she quickly gets into the car. He stands in her way to block her from leaving. Dodging him, she drives off as he jumps out of her way. Jack runs to his car and follows her. Sophia pulls up at the garage gate.

Sophia
Rajin, keep him waiting. I don't want him following me.

Rajin
Sure, Ma'am.

She exits the car park and the gate closes behind her. Jack's car pulls up hastily.

Jack
What's going on?

Rajin
Sorry, Sir, it's not opening.

Jack
Rajin, open it.

Rajin
It's not working.

Jack
Rajin, I will break it, I swear.

Rajin pretends to try to open the barrier but it's not working. Jack backs up his car and speeds forward as if he is going to break it. Rajin opens the barrier just in time and Jack drives away. Jack quickly catches up with Sophia's car and starts honking incessantly, tailing her for a while.

Sophia sees a police car ahead, with two officers in it, parked by the side of the road. She drives up beside them and Jack stops behind her. He thinks Sophia has pulled over to talk to him, so he gets out of the car.

Sophia
Good evening

Police
Good evening, Ma'am.

Sophia
Sir, this guy is stalking me.
Can you please do something about it?

Police
Sure, Ma'am.

They get out of their car and walk toward Jack. Sophia drives off waving at Jack as she watches the police officers checking his papers in her rearview mirror.

Jack
I am not a stalker! I swear she's my wife!!

Scene 11
The Avalon restaurant

Sophia arrives at the table where William is already waiting for her.

Sophia
Bonsoir

He stands up, pulls out the chair for her to sit, and then returns to his chair.

William
You're late.

She looks at her watch.

Sophia
It's 8:30 p.m. exactly!

William
My watch says 8:35 p.m.! Give me your watch.

Sophia
Excuse me?!

William
Your watch.

She gives him her watch. He takes it and adjusts her watch to exactly match his own.

William
If we're going to work together, you have to be on my time.

He hands her back the watch while she is still baffled by what just happened. A waiter appears holding a bottle of wine, which he presents to William.

Waiter
Chablis Grand Cru.

He pours a little for William to taste.

Waiter
Should I start with the food?

Sophia
Can I see the menu, please?

William
I ordered for you.

He nods at the waiter to pour Sophia some wine while she is wrapping her head around the situation. She thinks: "What a control freak this guy is!"

Cut to

One hour later

They've already finished the first two courses and their plates are empty in front of them. William is checking the plans while Sophia explains them.

Sophia
...and in the library, we would introduce touches of mother-of-pearl.

William
I like mother-of-pearl, but isn't it too Art Deco?

Sophia
Depends on how you use it. On the contrary, the addition of this element to the dark stainless steel will give a touch of shine to the main elements which are matte.

William
Hmm!! Won't it give the impression of being a bit too "soft"?

Sophia
Not at all! It's like saying that a man is very manly, yet compassionate. Unless that's not you!

William smiles in appreciation of her witty comment. The waiter returns with two plates of truffle risotto.

Sophia
The books in the library, are they decorative or...?

William
Or...

Sophia
Wow

William
Don't you read?

Sophia
Times have changed. Nowadays, if you need an answer to anything, you just Google it.

William
Answers?!

William laughs.

On the contrary, a good book entices you to ask questions. You are a beautiful woman and not wanting in any way. Try to stand out from the crowd.
A beautiful flower catches the eye, but a scented one lingers in your memory.

Sophia blushes and tries the truffle risotto. She is obviously impressed by the taste.

Sophia
Mmm!! So, what do you do for a living?

William
Me? I invest in extraordinary things.

Sophia
Like what?

William
Like, what you're eating.

Sophia
Risotto?!

William
It's what's on the risotto.

Sophia
Truffle?

William
White truffle.

Sophia
That's your job?

William nods in confirmation.

Sophia
You're telling me that you make this kind of a living out of truffle?!

William
What do you mean by "this kind of living"?

Sophia
Well, it's clear that you have a hard time making ends meet.

They both laugh.

William
I do many things. But do you have any idea how much a handful of this costs?

Sophia
Fifty dollars?

William
Add a couple of zeroes.

Sophia chokes on a mouthful of risotto when she hears the price.

Sophia
Five thousand????

William
And truffle is almost impossible to find.
It's even more expensive on the black market.

William
I can tell that you're passionate about what you do, too.

Sophia
Yes...that was before I found out that a handful of truffles cost five thousand dollars.

William laughs at her comment and holds up his glass.

William
Cheers, Miss Dagher!

Sophia
Mrs...

William
Oooohh! You're married?!

She nods... with some hesitation.

Sophia
Maybe...I'm not sure.

William
You're not sure! Interesting! Why don't you Google that?!

Cut to

At the end of their dinner meeting, they walk to the entrance of the Avalon.

William
So, are you done with the plans?

Sophia smiles coyly.

Sophia
Yesterday.

They both laugh.

Sophia
I'll work on the changes tomorrow,
so they'll be ready the day after.

William
10 a.m. My place.

The valet appears with Sophia's car.

William
Good night

Scene 12

Jack's private clinic at day

Jack is working on a patient, pulling his leg.
Distracted by his own thoughts, he pulls a little too hard.

Patient
Ohhhh!

Jack
Sorry

Rabih stands at the door.

Rabih
Can I have a word?

Jack goes to him.

As your wife's gynecologist, I'd like to remind you that she is currently ovulating. That means today is "showtime" for you, that is if you want to make a baby.

Jack
Super! Is there a specific time you're going to give me as well? Why don't you put a switch on me?
Horny on, horny off!

Rabih
If you need a cheering squad, we're ready.

Jack
Kiss my ass.

Rabih
What are you doing tonight?
Come over and watch the game.

Jack
Dunno...we'll talk.

Rabih starts to leave and smirks.

Rabih
Who's getting some tonight?

Jack pretends he's going to kick him and Rabih rushes out the door.

Scene 13

Yoga studio at night

Sophia is sitting in her regular spot in yoga class.
Jack enters wearing gym clothes with a towel on one shoulder.
He sits on the floor besides Sophia.

Sophia
What are you doing here?!

Jack
Yoga!

Sophia
Jack!

Jack
You're not answering my calls and I don't want to go to your mother's house.

The yoga teacher announces that the class is starting.
Jack tries to perform a yoga move but it turns out ridiculous.

Jack
Rabih says that you are ovulating now and that we should do it tonight.

Sophia
Great! Do it with Rabih!

Jack
Don't be silly!

The yoga teacher opens one eye and shoots Jack a stern look. Jack lifts his arms above his head in tree pose pretending to meditate.

He whispers again to Sophia when the teacher closes her eyes.

Jack
So? Sophia?

Sophia
You're seriously talking about this now?! Here?!

Jack
I thought you'd be relaxed here.

Sophia doesn't answer. She tries to control her temper.
Jack inhales – yoga style.

Sophia
Jack! Leave!

Jack
Promise me you'll finish and come home.

Sophia
What planet are you living on?! Seriously?!
Didn't you notice that I moved out?! Don't you get it?
And you're here talking to me about having a baby?!

Jack
Isn't that what you wanted?!

Jack tries a difficult move that the whole class is doing.

Sophia
Yes...but even animals perform a little dance before they do it! Fix your problems before you offer your services.

The yoga teacher opens her eyes once again.

Yoga teacher
Sir, you have to leave!

Jack
Why? I'm in the moment.

Jack is in a complicated stretching position. Sophia stands up.

Sophia
No, no, let him stay...

Sophia presses hard on his back, Jack pulls a muscle at the back of his leg.

Jack
Ohhh!

Sophia
...since he is in the moment!

Sophia leaves while Jack is still on the floor in pain.

Scene 14
William's house

Sophia rings the doorbell. The housekeeper lets her in.

Sophia
Good morning

Housekeeper
Good morning, Ma'am

Sophia enters.

Sophia
Is Mr. William here?

Sophia takes a glimpse at herself in the mirror and fixes her hair. She notices a striking bouquet of flowers on the credenza. She feels a petal and then takes a photo of the flowers. William arrives, in a suit, ready to leave.

William
Good morning

Sophia
Hello

William
Sorry, I have an urgent appointment. I have to be downtown in thirty minutes. We can postpone or you can come along and brief me on the way.

Sophia
You'll never make it... there's a lot of traffic.

William
Yee, of little faith...

Scene 15
William's yacht at sea

William and Sophia are in his large luxury yacht speeding toward Beirut.

Sophia
This is the first time I've made a presentation at sea!

William
Time is money.

William is looking at the plans as Sophia is explaining them to him. His phone rings.

William
Excuse me.

William answers the phone.

Yes, Tony?

Scene 16

Meeting room in a luxury office

Tony is in the conference room.
The board meeting has already convened.
He's standing aside and talking in a low voice.

Tony
Where are you?

William
Almost there. What's the matter with you?
Why are you always so anxious?

Tony
Something's not right.

William
Relax, this company will get sold to whom I want
at the price I set. Let them dream on.
They have no quorum to overrule my decision.

Tony
Selim is here.

William
Selim gave us power of attorney.

Tony
Not if he attends the meeting in person.

William is quiet.

Tony
I'm not comfortable, William. Something seems fishy.

The yacht reaches Zeitouna Bay Port in downtown Beirut.

William
I'm on my way.

He ends the call.

Sophia
Problems at work?

William
A bit of suspense but in the end, the hero always wins.

Sophia laughs. The yacht is almost docked.
William gets ready to get off the yacht, then stops for a moment.

William
What are you doing tonight? Come over.

Sophia
Thank you, but I can't.

William
I'm having a gathering and there are some people you should meet.

Sophia
I have plans already.

William
Cancel them.

Sophia
I don't think so.

William
Do you want to stay as an employee forever?!
The people you're going to meet tonight can change your life. Be there at 8:30 p.m. sharp and bring your ambitions with you.

Scene 17

Meeting room in a luxury office

William is chairing the meeting. The rest of the ten-member board is convened. Jamal, a member of the board, spearheads the opposition against William.

Jamal
The buyers have one hundred million dollars on the table. The majority of the board members have agreed to the sale.

Jamal pulls out a document.

Here are their signatures.

William
One hundred million!! You like it cheap.
This company is worth much more than that!

Jamal
Not in these tough times, especially with the liquidity crisis. Let me tell you what your problem is, William. You're still living in the glorious past.

William
At least I have a glorious past!
One that you have all benefitted from.

Selim
William, nobody is undermining your years of effort, but times have changed.

William
Selim, you most of all, know that when the deal is signed with the Chinese, the shares will skyrocket again!

Selim
It's been six months of you trying to close this "deal" and it hasn't happened.

William
Exactly Selim, times are no longer what they used to be. The deal requires much more effort, but it's going to happen – it's just a matter of time.

Selim
I don't have time. I lost a lot of money in the stock exchange and I need cash.

Scene 18

William's house at night

Twelve people are gathered around the pool. William is having a conversation with Tony.

William
We know that Jamal is doing everything in his power to become the chair. But what's in it for Selim?

Tony
Cash?

William
He's lying. He personally told me that the last thing he would ever invest in, is the stock exchange. I'm sure Jamal has promised him something.

Sophia shows up at the door looking gorgeous. William approaches her and smiles jokingly.

William
You're late.

Sophia shows him her wrist.

Sophia
I changed watches.

William
You look great.

Sophia
Thank you.

William
Come and let me introduce you.

William
Dr. Salman needs no introduction.
And Dr. Omar is the founder and CEO of the Children's Cancer Center. Or should I already call you, your Excellency, Minister of Health?!

Dr. Omar
How did you know?!

William
Never mind. And it suits you very well.
By the way, this is Sophia, a first-class interior decorator. She has a refined and elegant taste and is working on my house.

Sophia
Pleased to meet you.

Dr. Omar
Wonderful! She can decorate the new children's rooms at the center.

William
Wow! That fast, your Excellency?!

Dr. Omar
William, if you say she's good, then she's excellent.
I know your standards.

William
Thank you, doctor.

Sophia
William likes to exaggerate things.

They laugh. A waiter enters carrying a tray of champagne flutes. William takes two glasses of champagne and offers one to Sophia.

The song "Temptation" by Michelle Gurevich plays in the background.*

William whispers to Sophia

*scan to play the song

William
Show some self-confidence, please!

Sophia
Self-confidence I have, but your ego... I don't!

William
You're mistaken...they are two sides of the same coin. You have more ego than I do. In fact, you have so many dormant talents and I'm going to awaken them...Cheers!

William holds up his glass.
Sophia looks at him for a moment and shakes her head.
Then, she holds her glass high for a toast.

Sophia
Cheers!

The party continues late into the night.

From a distance, William observes Sophia talking to another guest, he watches her delicate hands gesture while she chats. The corners of her mouth curve upward as she smiles politely while intently engaged in discussion. She pauses and turns to meet William's gaze

fade to black

Scene 19

William's house

William is in the pool for his morning swim. His friend, Dr. Fouad (50 years old) arrives and waits for him to finish.

After climbing out of the pool, William walks to the breakfast bar where a bowl of apples and breakfast is freshly laid out.

He picks up two cups of coffee, hands one to Dr. Fouad, and sits facing him.

William
No work today?

Dr. Fouad
I do have work but I wanted to see you.
How are you?

William
Doing well. I'm going to China tomorrow, wanna come?

Dr. Fouad shakes his head.

William
Please come. I'll feed you chicken leg soup. It's a special treat.

Dr. Fouad
I can't go... and neither can you.

William
Why so?

Dr. Fouad
The result of the biopsy came out.
And the nodule we thought was a cyst...it's not a cyst.

William
What is it then?

Dr. Fouad stays silent, looking pensive.

William
Fouad?! Speak up! As bad as it is, it can't be worse than your silence. Speak!!

Dr. Fouad
It's cancer.

William
How bad?

Dr. Fouad
Bad.

William
How bad?!

Dr. Fouad looks away and doesn't answer.

William
Speak!!!

Dr. Fouad
Stage four. The worst.

Time slows down.
William's mind races.
He sees a series of flashbacks in quick succession:
Lying in the MRI machine,
Swimming underwater in a pool,
A baby being born,
His mother calling him when he was a child,
Punching a boxing bag,
Making love to a beautiful woman,
A child is sitting in a handmade wooden cart on tiny wheels, speeding downhill heading straight for a wall. The child screams and closes his eyes.

Cut to black

four months later

William is in his chair, tired and weak.
A few books lie beside him on the table.
Dr. Fouad sits near him in the same place as four months ago.

Dr. Fouad
Are you getting into the water at all?

William
No.

Dr. Fouad
But Willy, getting some exercise is good for you.
Mateo can help you.

William
You want me to splash around when I used to rule the pool?!

Dr. Fouad
But these exercises will make you stronger.

Mateo (30 years old), William's well-built gay nurse, appears carrying a cup of coffee for Dr. Fouad.

William
Make me stronger for what?
To prolong my suffering?!
Doctors are amazing creatures!
A patient is dying and instead of finishing him off quickly, they enjoy grilling him on a slow fire.

William flips his hand back and forth, imitating a steak being grilled.

Rare? Medium? Well-done?

Dr. Fouad and Mateo laugh.

William
If you want to be of service to me, give me some more morphine. At least that will quiet the noises I hear in my head.

Mateo
Yes, yes, please doctor, the noises are so loud I can even hear them myself. And throw in some mary jane while you're at it.

They laugh.

William
Seriously speaking, I need to occupy myself with something!

Dr. Fouad
Anyway, you're too idle. You need a physiotherapist.
I know an excellent one. It's good for you and it'll keep you busy.
I'll send him by.

William
You'll send "her" by.

Mateo
The doctor said he'll send him by.

William
A woman! Tall, blonde with big boobs...

Mateo
...whose name is Youssef.

William is in deep thought and then seems to have gotten an idea...

William
I know exactly who you are going to send!

Scene 20
William's house

Jack parks his car in William's driveway.

Cut to

On the terrace, William is stretched out on a couch reading a book, beside him is a bottle of XO cognac.
He is sipping on a glass while smoking a cigarillo. Mateo arrives.

Mateo
Non, non, non.

William
Si, si, si.

William picks up a photograph to use as a bookmark and then sets the book aside.

Mateo
You're completely nuts!

William
And what should I be afraid of? Getting cancer?

Mateo
My God, William!

William
Come, sit and drink to my health.

Mateo sits beside him.

Mateo
No, no, I don't like it.

William
Come on!

William holds the glass to Mateo's mouth.
Mateo takes the glass, smells the cognac before having a tiny sip, and makes a face because of its strong taste.

Mateo
Hmm

William, holding out a cigarillo, motions to Mateo.

William
Come on.

Mateo, still struggling with the taste of the cognac, shakes his finger refusing the cigarillo.

William
Come on!

Mateo concedes and takes a puff. He starts coughing and his eyes water, while William laughs at him.

Cut to

In the driveway, Jack has gotten out of the car and is taking his time to admire the house and the garden.
He slowly walks to the door and rings the bell.

Cut back

The housekeeper appears in front of William.

Housekeeper
Sir, there's a guy at the door "for massage."

William flings his hand up.

William
In the garbage!

The housekeeper puts her hand over her mouth and chuckles at William's answer.

Mateo follows the housekeeper to welcome Jack in.

Jack is standing in the living room taking everything in.
His eyes scan the paintings and the decor: a cigar box, telescope, statue of a naked woman, cognac carafe, and a giant bookcase.
Jack lightly passes his finger over the breast of the naked woman.

Mateo
Hello

Startled, Jack quickly takes his hand away from the statue's breast as Mateo laughs.

Jack
Hello

Mateo
I'm Mr. William's nurse. Please follow me.

Jack steps out onto the terrace and is surprised to see William drinking and smoking.

Jack
Hello

William
Hello

Jack
Mr. William?

William has a frown on his face.

William
Yes?

Jack
Dr. Fouad asked me to come.

William
Concerning the toilet that's running?
Mateo, show him where the toilet is.

Jack is taken aback.

Jack
I'm not the plumber, I'm the physiotherapist.
The doctor told me to come for someone who is ill, is that you?

William
Do you see anything wrong with me?
I'm smoking and having a cognac.

Jack
Hmmm No...Yes

William
Why are you stuttering? Pull yourself together!

Mateo laughs and comes to Jack's rescue.

Mateo
William, stop it!

Jack is dumbfounded and remains a bit hesitant before taking a seat.

Mateo
What would you like to drink?

Jack
Thanks, but I don't want to trouble you.

William
What do you mean, you don't want to trouble him?
Mateo, bring him something...bring him some yogurt.

Jack is taken aback once again when he hears that William wants to offer him yogurt. He turns and looks at Mateo wondering if William is being serious.

Jack
Really, I can't.

William
Of course, you can. It's fresh and great for the intestines.

Jack
No really, thank you.

William
You're having the yogurt.

Mateo
Naughty William.

Cut to

Scene 21
Interior design office

Sophia is at her desk working and hears a knock on the door. A delivery man comes in carrying a bouquet of flowers.

Delivery man
Madame Sophia?

Sophia
Yes?

Delivery man
Sign here, please.

Sophia signs and the delivery man puts the bouquet down on her desk.

Sophia
No card?

Delivery man
I don't have a clue, Ma'am.

Scene 22
William's house, his bedroom

William is lying on a foldable massage bed that Jack has brought. Jack is moving William's arms and legs.

William
You work, what... seven, eight hours a day?

Jack
More.

William
Your girlfriend is very lucky, she must get a daily massage.

Jack
My wife.

William
And you have an excuse to rub her neck every day.

Jack smiles at the thought.

William
They need a good neck wringing, right?

Jack doesn't answer.

William
With those hands, she must idolize you.

Jack
She idolizes me so much that she has left me.

William
Should I congratulate or console you on that?

Jack
Excuse me?!

William
Sorry, but if you have an unbearable wife, then good riddance.

A sudden sadness comes over Jack, as he remembers his problems with Sophia.

William
But...if you still love her then it's a problem.

Jack perks up his head and quickly answers without thinking.

Jack
I certainly do.

William
Are you sure?!

Jack
Yes, very sure!

William
Could it be that you have grown accustomed to her? People often confuse love with habit.

Jack
No, I am certain. I do love her.

William
So, if I ask you what you love the most about her, what is the first thing that comes to your mind?

Few seconds pass by. Jack can't find an answer.

William
Hmmmm! Okay... and how about her? Sorry I'm asking, if you'd rather not answer, I'd understand.

Jack
No, no problem. What about her?

William
Why did she leave? Does she have somebody else?

Jack
NO WAY!

William observes him, sizing up the gravity of Jack's oblivion. Jack can feel William's eyes on him.

Jack
What?!

William
Nothing.

Jack
No, say what you have to say.

William
Nothing, I just like the overdose of self-confidence that you radiate.

Jack
It's not an overdose of self-confidence. She's my wife and I know her by heart.

William
Hmm! I am in the presence of a man who knows women by heart!

Jack
Well, I do know her by heart.

Willam
Seriously?! So why are you divorcing then?!
Don't take her for granted, my friend.
A woman's software is completely different from a man's. Your computer may read the code but not decipher it.

Cut to

Scene 23
Interior design office

Sophia contemplates the bouquet as if remembering something. She grabs her phone and goes through her photo gallery. She stops at the photo of the bouquet that she took at William's house; it's the same.

After a few moments, she decides to call William. The call doesn't go through, as if he blocked her number.

Scene 24
William's house

Mateo is showing Jack to the door. The sound of William coughing comes from another room.

Jack
I tried to clear his lungs. But you can't let him smoke, it's suicidal.

Mateo
He doesn't listen.

Jack
And chemo? Is he undertaking treatment?

Mateo
He refuses.

Jack
Anyway, let him rest. The first session is always a tough one.

Scene 25
Fishing boat docked at night

Nady and Rabih are waiting on the boat. Jack rushes onboard carrying his things.

Nady
Where have you been, bro?

Jack
Sorry, Sorry, Sorry! But I have this new patient, a smart-ass. He held me up with his theories and philosophical remarks.

Jack places his phone in the box next to the captain's seat, along with the others.

Jack
I'm going down to change.

Nady tries to start the boat's engine in vain.

Cut to

An hour later

Unable to start the boat, they remain in the port.
They are drinking beer and eating pizza. Jack looks pensive.

Rabih
Hello?! Earth to Jack!

Jack
I'm thinking about my patient.
He's got shit loads of money, a villa with a pool to die for.
Then, out of nowhere, he's got cancer. Bam, his life is over!

Nady
You're such a drama queen!

Jack
If you were told that you have six months to live, what would you do?

Nady
The first thing I'd do is block my wife so she doesn't bug me anymore. Then I'd fill this boat with booze and women and die drunk between their thighs!

Jack
You're so stupid!

Nady
Bro, why do you want to spoil our evening? Did I give the man cancer? Sophia is right to want to leave you!!

Jack
Eat shit!

Rabih
What's new with you two?

Jack
What's new?! A duo album and a divorce agreement.

Rabih
Oh, by the way. I ran into your boss, Nabil.
He told me he's immigrating to Canada and that they are seriously considering you to replace him as Head of the Physio Department.

Jack
Woohoooo! Yessss! Actually, I just remembered he sent me a WhatsApp message today and I completely forgot to read it.

Nady is standing beside the box where they all place their phones.

Jack
Nady, can you hand me my phone so I can check it?

Jack, who is still celebrating, doesn't notice Nady winking at Rabih before taking a phone and throwing it at him really quickly.

Nady
Here, catch!

Jack, who wasn't paying attention, doesn't catch the phone in time and it goes over the boat into the water.
Jack, furious, is running back and forth screaming at Nady.

In the meantime, Nady and Rabih are playing it cool.

Rabih
Man, why did you do that?

Nady
It's his fault... he wasn't looking.

Jack
It's my fault!! You idiot, I've told you a million times not to throw my phone!!

Nady
Please Jack... just charge me for it, but stop nagging about it!

In the meantime, Jack plunges a fishing net into the water and is frantically trying to fish out the phone.

At that sight, Nady and Rabih can't hold it in anymore and burst out laughing.

Realizing that it's all a prank, Jack attacks them both, throwing punches.

Jack
What did you throw in the water?!

Nady
A fake phone.

Nady hands Jack his phone. He punches Nady on the shoulder.

Jack
Prick.

Scene 26

Jack and Sophia's favorite coffee shop

The camera pans a cozy coffee shop with couches to sink into and dim lighting from vintage lamps.
A few people huddle in intimate groups, chatting.

Jack (Off screen)
Can we have a coffee together?

Sophia (Off screen)
Why?

Jack (Off screen)
I need to talk to you.

Sophia is silent for a moment.

Sophia (Off screen)
I don't know if I'm up to it.

Jack (Off screen)
Please...I'm asking you to.

Jack and Sophia are seated in a corner at the far end of the coffee shop. Jack is sipping his coffee.
Sophia is finishing a glass of wine.

Sophia
Waiter, please, another one.

Jack
It's your third!

Sophia
Other than to ask about my health, my mom

and my work, why did you bring me here?

Jack
Because this used to be our hangout place.
We had our first coffee here together.

Sophia
I know, I never stopped coming here.
But you, this place just dawned on you?

Jack hesitates. He doesn't know where to start.

Sophia
Go ahead, spill the beans!

Jack
Do you still love me?

Sophia pauses

Sophia
I don't know.

Jack
You don't know?! Who knows, then?

Sophia
I don't know who knows. Do you?

Jack
I do!

Sophia
Well, I was your wife, I witnessed our life together.

Jack
And?

Sophia
You were never there.

Jack
What are you talking about?! I was always there.

Sophia
Crashed out on the sofa in front of the TV doesn't count.
You were distant, very distant, careless with zero emotions! ...You come home very late at night, almost always with a headache, ignoring any word I say, yearning for your beer to relax.

Jack
Because I come back from work exhausted!

Sophia
On Saturdays, you have your doctorate courses.
Okay, fine. I'm all for you being ambitious.
Actually, it's one of the reasons I fell for you.
On Sundays, I beg you to go out somewhere. You're tired,
and it's too "hot," or too "cold."
You just wanna watch TV all day.

She imitates the zombie-like movement of pressing the remote control.

Click, click... You even know all the names of the
third-division football players.

Jack
Sunday is the only day where I get to stretch out my legs!
Aren't I entitled to relax after a long week?
Crucify me for that Sophia, crucify me!!

Tension starts to rise.

Sophia
Am I crucifying you?! I wonder who's doing it to whom?!
When I went for the procedure after the miscarriage,
were you with me?! Whose baby was I carrying in my womb?!

Jack
Your mother was with you. What were we all going to do
at the hospital?!

Sophia
I didn't want my mom, I wanted you to be there.
Do I have a man beside me or not?!

Jack
Yes! You do have a man, a man you never listened to.
Maybe if you had listened, the baby wouldn't have died.
I told you: "Sophia take it easy, Sophia please rest!!"
But NO! You wanted to move into a new house and do
everything yourself including the entire renovation!

Sophia
The tiny pigsty we were living in barely fit the two of us!
Where would the baby sleep? Where would I put his stuff?
Tell me?! Maybe if you had lifted a finger to help me fix
the house, then our baby would still be alive!

Jack
Because I do nothing all day, right?
I don't work my ass off!

Sophia
As if you're the only one with a job? I work too, plus I go
to the supermarket, make dinner, and move houses!

Sophia falls silent for a moment.

I'm tired of quarreling with you Jack, I really am.
We're not on the same wavelength.
Maybe it's just better that we both have a fresh start with the right person.

Scene 27

William's house, his bedroom

Brazilian bossa nova music is playing in the background.
Lying on the bed, William inhales and exhales into a spirometer,[2] a small blue plastic ball goes up and falls, then goes up again.

Jack stands by his side.

Jack
Try to keep the ball high for as long as you can, rest, and then, blow it back up again. You should do this all the time, it opens up your lungs.

William
It needs a piece of charcoal.

Jack cracks a smile.

Jack
You're doing excellent today,
I can see gradual improvement.

William
Good news. Where's the party?

Jack barely smiles again.

William
What's the matter? Are you going to a funeral?!

Jack
She went out with someone.

William
Good, good, I'm happy for her.
But who are we talking about?

Jack
Sophia, my wife. Turns out there's another man.

2 In Lebanese Arabic, a spirometer is called an argileh.

William
Oh!

William pauses.

How did you find out?

flashback

Scene 28

Jack and Sophia's favorite coffee shop

Jack
...the right person?! So, have you found that person?

Sophia shakes her head.

Jack
Are you sure?!

Jack stares at Sophia, trying to read her.

Your eyes are saying different.

Sophia
I don't have someone else.

Sophia speaks calmly, although engrossed in her thoughts.

But I did go out with someone.

Jack
You dated someone!!!

Sophia nods.

And you slept with him??

Sophia rolls her eyes, as if summoning divine patience.

Jack
Did you?

Sophia
That's all you care about?!

Jack
Answer the question!

The tension rises.

Sophia
What difference does it make?!

Jack
It makes a huge difference!

Sophia
It's been more than four months since I moved out.
We already started the divorce formalities.
We disagree over the color of the sky.
What do you care if I slept with him or not?!

Jack
I care more than you know! And FYI we are still married.
You're still registered under my name!

Sophia
Registered!! Am I a car? Registered in his name!
You know what? Yes! I did sleep with him!
And it was amazing!

Sophia grabs her bag and gets up to leave.

Sophia
Make sure you sign the divorce papers first thing
tomorrow morning, and don't you dare tell me
"I want to think about it."
Thinking is not one of your virtues.

Sophia leaves. Jack punches the table.

Flashback ends

The small blue plastic ball is still going up then falling, then going up again.

Now Jack is lying on the bed blowing into the spirometer in despair.

William stands beside him with an amused smile on his face, and pats him on the shoulder in sympathy

William
Try another blow...it'll relieve you.

Jack
Ahhhh!!

William
Blow, blow, it will help you relax.

Jack
Do you think he knows me?

William

William takes on a jokingly sarcastic tone.

And you've given him a massage as well.
Man, why are you torturing yourself with those thoughts?!

Jack
What do you want me to think about?!
How many eggs go into a cake?!
I'm telling you my wife slept with someone else!

William
But she left you and asked for a divorce.

Jack
Maybe she left home but she's still my wife.

William
On paper!

Jack
She is still my wife!!

*

The bossa nova song "Voce vai ver" is playing in the background.*

William
Let's set one thing straight.
Since you already lost her, then it's a matter of ego!

Jack
Listen, I wanted to tell you this many times, but I held back.
You know what I hate most? I hate people who give their opinion about things that they have never experienced.
You're the king of empty talk!
First, live with a woman under the same roof before you become a relationship coach!

William
And you are the king at burying your head in the sand!
Classic, as soon as a sensitive topic is brought up you start shooting arrows.

Jack
And you are the king of theorizing!!

William
Maybe. But it's not me who has problems with my wife.
Jack, you don't listen! Question: Is your wife a slut?!

Jack ignores William.

What do you think pushed her to this point?

Jack doesn't answer.

I asked you before and I'm asking you again:

Why do you love her?

Jack is indignant.

Jack?

Jack
Sorry, but I'm not taking lessons from a spectator.

William
Do you think I need to be a Michelin star chef to tell the taste of good food?!

Jack

Jack begins to sing Dalida's song.

Parole, Parole, Parole[3]

William
Isn't it possible that I know so much about marriage that I chose not to get married?!

Jack
Parole, Parole, Parole

William is silent for a moment looking around the room.
He pauses on some old vinyl records stashed on the shelves.
He decides to tell Jack a story.

William
I met the most beautiful woman in Cyprus...

Flashback

Scene 29
Cyprus Hotel at night

A Suzuki Landy moped arrives at the hotel entrance with four people squeezed on it.
A man is steering it; a girl is sitting behind him on the seat;

William (37 years old) is sitting on the rear metal pad, and behind him is Dr. Fouad dangling in the air,

3 (Blah, Blah, blah)

his hands are on William's waist who, in turn, is holding him by the legs. They're all tipsy.

When the moped stops, William gets off. He is wearing a suit without a tie and he looks disheveled.

William
One more drink.

Driver
Not a drop.

William
Please!!

Girl
Bye, Willy!

The moped takes off.

Dr. Fouad
Ela re

William
Ela re

The rest
Ela re

William
Ela re

William arrives at the hotel bar. The place is almost empty except for one table. The pianist is playing "Voce vai ver."

On the bar, there's a Brazilian passport, a book, and a glass of champagne. The bartender is preparing a drink.

Upon William's arrival, the bartender smiles and talks to him in English with a Cypriot accent.

William
Scotch, please

Bartender
Here you go, Sir.

William
Got a match?

Bartender
Sorry

William
I can't get a light in a hotel bar?! If it weren't for us, you'd still be riding donkeys!

William takes a sip of his drink and turns to see who else is at the bar. He looks at the pianist and does a double take as if something unusual caught his eye.

At a closer glance, he sees a beautiful woman lying on the floor under the piano.

William, feeling tipsy, looks at his drink, blinks, then looks back under the piano. The woman is still there.

William
Do you see someone under the piano or is it just me?!

The bartender motions toward the Brazilian passport and the champagne glass sitting on the bar.

Bartender
This lady is lying there.

William
Interesting!

William goes to the piano and bends down to talk to her. Miuca (32 years old, beautiful and eccentric) has her eyes closed and is entranced by the melody.

William
Hello

Miuca

Miuca opens her eyes.

Hi

William
How's the weather down there?

Miuca
Come and check it out for yourself.

William hesitates for a second and then lies down next to her under the piano.

William
Any chance of rain? Is that why you hid here?

Miuca
I was just listening to the music.

William
What's wrong with listening from over there?

Miuca
If you close your eyes and listen, you'd know the difference.

William closes his eyes and listens. His face fills with emotions. He opens his eyes.

William
Wow!!

Miuca
You feel the sound vibrations with your body.
It impacts you both emotionally and physically.
It's proven to reduce stress and anxiety.

William
It's true!

William looks at the pianist's legs and waist right above him.

William
Let's hope that the guy didn't have beans
for lunch.

Miuca looks at him and they burst out laughing.

Flashback ends

Jack

Jack is laughing.

Under the piano?!

William
Under the piano!!

Jack
What did you say her name was?

Flashback continues

William and Miuca walk back to their seats.

William
I'm William.

Miuca
Miuca.

William
Miuca! Interesting name.

Miuca
It's Brazilian.

Bartender
Sorry, to interrupt but we're closing in a minute.

William

William is irritated and turns to the bartender, speaking in Arabic.

Hala2 fe2et tsakir ya charmout.[4]

Bartender
Excuse me?!

William

William smiles at him.

Thank you, has tizi.

Bartender
Has tizi?!

William
Yeah, it's Lebanese brown pudding, very intense.
Perfect for you.

Bartender
Nice.

William and Miuca leave the bar which is close to the sea.

William
Let's walk.

Miuca looks down at her dress and her high heels and jokingly smiles.

Miuca
Perfect outfit!

William kneels in front of her, holds up her foot, and removes one of her shoes while looking into her eyes. She is surprised, at first, but then smiles and kicks off the second shoe. It flies off.

He jumps down from the ledge to the sand and holds out his hand to help her. She holds on to him and jumps down.

A cell phone rings.

Flashback ends

4 Roughly translated to: "Now you choose to close, bitch!?"

Jack's phone begins to ring, interrupting William. Startled, he fumbles around for his phone in his pocket and answers.

Jack
Ela re, Salwa? Uhh, yes, Salwa? I'm on my way.

Jack hangs up his phone.

I'm late for my next appointment.

Jack gets up to leave.

William
Are you seeing her at all?

Jack
She's not talking to me! The last time we met it went really bad.

William
Hmm, is there someone else that you both know who would like to see you back together?

Jack understands what William insinuated.

Scene 30

Jihane's house

Sophia and Jihane are arguing.

Jihane
...yes, I invited him over to dinner.
What's the problem with that?
Jack is an ambitious guy from a good family.
I know he has his faults...maybe he's a bit harsh sometimes?
But all men have faults, Sophia. Don't think that you'll ever find the perfect man.

Sophia
Mom, stay out of it!

Jihane
You've been telling me not to get involved all along, and look where that got us. If I don't try to do something now, then when?!

Sophia
I wish you had tried to do something about your relationship

with Dad, instead of lecturing me! Or were you also looking for the perfect man?!

Jihane
Now isn't the time to talk about why your father left!
But at least I was married for ten years. I had a child and I did try hard. While you just got into it.
After only two years of marriage, and you're already getting divorced!

Sophia
I'm learning from you, Mama. Isn't that better than having a child and having it grow up fatherless?!

Jihane is taken aback by Sophia's harsh words.
Sophia is sorry for what she said.

She goes to Jihane and holds her hand.

Sophia
I'm sorry, Mama. I didn't mean that.

Sophia pauses.

Okay, I'll give him another chance, for you.

Scene 31
William's house

William and Tony are seated by the pool.

Tony
...the deal with the Chinese is called off.
They sent an official response that they're out.

William
I'm not surprised. Jamal did everything to push them out.
And that's what happened.

Tony
But I don't get his reason.
He has shares in the company as well.
And he was dying to sell!

William
Tony, dear, a major variable has changed.
Soon I'll be gone but not my shares.

They will be sold at auction and the board members will have the priority to bid. Only an idiot would increase their value before buying them.

Tony
And what do you plan on doing?!

William
Actually, I'm confused between black and white.

Tony
I don't get it.

William
The color of the coffin. What do you think?
Black is more royal, right?

Tony
Sorry, I know it's a sensitive topic, but the company has over two hundred employees and families living off it!

William
Do you think a lacquered black or matte finish is best?

Cut to

Scene 32

Interior design office

Sophia is working on a file. She stops and stares at the wilting bouquet.

After a pensive moment, she heads to the file cabinet, opens it, and goes through all the files until she finds William's.

She looks his landline number and dials it.

Housekeeper
Good morning.

Sophia
Hello, is Mr. William available?

Housekeeper
Who's calling?

Sophia
A friend.

Housekeeper
Sorry, Ma'am, I need a name please.

Sophia
Never mind.

Sophia hangs up. She grabs her handbag and leaves the office.

Cut back

Wearing a pair of swimming trunks and a t-shirt, Jack arrives with his physiotherapy equipment.

Jack
Bonjourno

Tony
Hello

William
That's a big bag today!

Jack
I have a surprise for you.

William
A gorgeous woman inside, maybe?

Tony
Then, I'll excuse myself...

William
Tony, do you remember when I used to tell you: "Time is money"? Well, forget about it. "Time is priceless." Go do what you love.

Tony, with a compassionate yet frustrated reaction, leaves. William is lost in his dark thoughts.

Jack tries to change William's mood.

He removes his shirt, takes out styrofoam dumbbells from the bag and throws himself in the pool.

Jack
Aquagym today. Ta daaa!

Jack makes an exercise-like movement in the water.

William
No pool for me.

Jack
Why?

William shakes his head.

Jack
But I have some really good news.

William
Tell it to me on dry land.

Jack
What's the matter with you today? Are you on your period?

William
Something like that.

Jack
If that's the case, better you don't swim, you'll dirty the pool.

William
Not bad!

Jack
Do you think you're the only one who knows how to offer yogurt?

William
You're happy today!

Jack
Come on, don't burst my bubble. Don't get in the water, just sit on the edge and let's chat. No need to exercise if you don't feel like it. But let's not go into your room, it's too depressing.

William stares at him blankly for a moment, then goes and sits at the edge of the pool with his legs in the water.

William
After you.

Jack
Nooo... Age before beauty!

William
I'm older, fine. But you, beauty?!

Jack
You're jealous.

William laughs.

You took a walk on the beach and then?

William
Which beach?

Jack
Ela re.

William
I run a kindergarten! And tell bedtime stories!

William finally chooses to continue telling his story.

Jack
Can we order some popcorn?

Jack shouts loudly.

Mateo, two popcorns, extra salt.

William laughs.

flashback

Scene 33

Sandy beach at night

William and Miuca are walking barefoot on the beach with their feet in the water. In the distance, a bonfire is lit, with people around it.

William
What brings a Brazilian girl to Cyprus?

Miuca
A wedding. You?

William
Meetings.

Miuca
What do you do?

William
Investments and funds, mainly.

Miuca
Ohh you're a golden boy.

William

William laughs.

Yes. And you?

Miuca
I'm not that shiny. I'm an artist.

William
Ouch! Where I come from, "artist" is a euphemism for prostitute. You'll have to be more specific.

Miuca

Miuca laughs.

A painter, I paint.

William
Nice. What do you paint?

Miuca

Miuca pauses.

My emotions.

William
And you have a lot of them, I bet.

Miuca

Miuca laughs again.

And very mixed ones.

William
Schizophrenic? Bipolar? Like, I love you for breakfast and hate you for lunch.

They laugh. They approach three couples sitting around the bonfire grilling hotdogs and marshmallows. Empty beer bottles are lying in the sand.

Girl 1
Beauty is...relative...

Guy 1
(Italian accent) Beauty is mamma mia.

Guy 2
My turn, my turn. The word is love, you start.

Girl 2
Oh, let's see. Love is, eh...a many splendored thing?

Guy 3
Love is a voluntary prison.

A marshmallow hits Guy 3, thrown by his girlfriend. William and Miuca reach the group.

William
Ela re

Guy 1
Ela re

Guy 2 offers each of them a marshmallow stick. They take it.

William
Thank you

Guy 2

Guy 2 looks at Miuca.

What's your definition of love?

Miuca is surprised at the question and hesitates.

Guy 2
We're playing a game. Come on!

Miuca
Love is...a miracle?

Guy 1
Bella, bella

Guy 1 sends her a kiss. Everyone looks at William.

William
Love?... Well, I haven't been there yet... but I intend to have a good answer by morning.

William looks at Miuca. They all start whistling and cheering.

Guy 1 raises William's arm in the air as if proclaiming him the winner.

Guy 1
Campione, campione.[5]

Flashback ends

William is still sitting on the edge of the pool. Jack is in the pool, moving William's legs.

Jack
Ahhh...when love roars!

William
Indeed! Never in my life had I gone crazy over a woman like that!

William slowly begins to do the exercise by himself. Jack corrects his moves. William follows instructions.

5 Meaning "champion, champion."

Jack
And did you discover true love?!

William
You know the saying: Love is degrading?

Jack laughs. William taps his chest.

It was ME, whom they were describing…

flashback

Scene 34

Cyprus Hotel at dawn

The elevator door opens and William and Miuca step out. They walk down a corridor until they get to Miuca's room.
She gives him back the jacket which was on her shoulders.

William
So, what do we do now?

Miuca
Sleeping is good for your skin.

He laughs. Through the window, they can see the sun beginning to rise.

William

Smiling coyly at her, William speaks in Arabic.

Fiyeh tal3ik 3a 2oudteh?
Baweslik 2asabi3 2ejraykeh wa7ad wa7ad?[6]

Miuca
What did you say?

William
3am 2oul eno 3abeleh fasefsik. Sem3a bel broasted? Badeh fasefsik mitel el broasted.[7]

Miuca
Well, not tonight.

William
But I'm leaving tomorrow, and ---!!!

Then he realizes that she understood what he said in Arabic.

6 Meaning: Can I take you to my room? And kiss your toes one by one?
7 I want to tear you apart like I would a broasted chicken. Have you ever heard of broasted?

His eyes widen as if someone just threw a bucket of icy water on him.

William is so embarrassed that he's unable to speak and makes gestures, pointing to the Brazilian passport that she's holding in her hand. He then starts to bang his forehead lightly on the wall.

William
How?!...oh God!!
What about the Brazilian passport and your name?!

Miuca

Miuca laughs.

Half the Brazilian population is originally Lebanese.

William holds his forehead with one hand and hits his other hand on the wall.

Flashback ends

Jack laughs loudly.

Jack
Whoa, my stomach! I can't take it anymore! Please!

William
Happy?! I'm entertaining you?

Jack
Fabulous! The most amazing story I've ever heard!

William
Indeed, if I had made it up, it wouldn't be as good!
Now, you tell me your good news.

Jack
I'm having dinner at her place tomorrow night.

William
Oh! How did that work out?

Jack
I'll tell you all about it, but first, dip your head in the water so you don't get a sunstroke.

William looks briefly at Jack before deciding to get into the pool. He then goes underwater. William's head is underwater with his eyes open.

At the far side of the pool, he sees two women. One is in her early sixties and the other is in her mid-forties.

William panics at this sight and moves his head instantly out of the water, coughing and gasping for air. Jack grabs him, trying to calm him down.

Jack
What's wrong?! What happened?!

William holds on to the edge of the pool trying to catch his breath.

Jack
William?!

William
Nothing...I'm okay, I just need to rest.

Sophia arrives in her car and parks it at a distance from William's house. She steps out of the car and walks toward the main gate.

William is stretched out on the couch in the living room and Jack is sitting facing him. Mateo holds a glass of water for William, who is feeling a bit stronger. William notices someone on the security app on his phone screen. He calmly takes a closer look. His suspicions are confirmed. It is Sophia walking toward the door!

William thinks quickly, trying to keep his composure, despite the seriousness of the situation.

William
Where are you parked?

Jack
Underground. Why are you asking?

William
Let me walk you to your car; I'll tell you on our way.

William gestures to Mateo to come closer.

Mateo?

Mateo approaches. William whispers a few words in his ear. Mateo leaves immediately.

The living room is made of huge glass windows that overlook the garden offering full visibility on both sides.

Mateo walks Sofia through the backyard skillfully, maneuvering and distratcing her from looking inside.

In sync, William gets up and walks Jack to his car engaging him with some story, making sure that his back is to the garden to avoid seeing Sophia.

Miraculously, Jack leaves without seeing Sophia, and vice versa. Mateo and Sophia are on the terrace. He gestures for Sophia to sit.

Sophia
...So, you bought the house?

Mateo
Yes.

Sophia
When exactly?

Mateo
About two months ago.

Sophia
And you know nothing about him?

Mateo
I bought it through a real estate agency.
I've never met the guy.

Silence falls between the two of them. Sophia turns away and notices an Audemars Piguet watch on the coffee table.

Sophia
When he sold you the house, did he also sell you his watch?!

Mateo
You mean this one! It's mine.

Sophia
Is it? Because he had the same one!

Mateo
Really?! A man after my own heart.
I'm beginning to like him.

Mateo pauses.

What are you doing tonight? Can I take you out?

The security camera on the ceiling moves very slightly.

Lying in his bed, William is watching the whole scene unfold on his phone through the security camera.

With his finger, William caresses Sophia's face.

Scene 35

Fishing boat at sunset

Sitting on the boat anchored at sea, Nady and Jack are drinking beer with their fishing rods in front of them.

Nady is texting on his phone.

Jack
The worst thing about Rabih's job is that it's unpredictable. He had an emergency so he had to cancel fishing.

Nady is talking to Jack while looking at WhatsApp.
His phone beeps warning him that the battery is almost empty.

Nady
You brought tears to my eyes! He probably made a thousand dollars on this...please!!!

Jack
Can you remove the damn phone from your hand?!

Nady
Chill! It's work! A Saudi gig.

At that moment, Nady's battery dies.

Nady
No. No. No!!.

Jack
What???

Nady
My phone's gone dead and I don't have a charger!

Jack
Thank God!! I'm going to the bathroom.

Jack goes down to the lower level. Immediately, Nady takes Jack's fishing rod and reels it in quickly.

Cut to

Scene 36
William's house

William is in his room, reading a book. He tires of reading and takes a photo of an empty hammock from the nearby table, and places it inside the book as a bookmark.

On one of the shelves in front of him is a photograph inside a silver frame. He stares at it. The photo is of the two women he saw at the bottom of the pool.

Cut back

Jack
Shall we leave? I don't want to be late for dinner.

Nady
Okay

Nady starts reeling in his fishing rod. Jack does the same but feels an unusual weight on his rod.

Jack
Nady, Nady, I caught something big!

Nady
Really?

Jack
Ohhh! I'm unable to pull it in, it's so heavy!

Nady
Hold on tight. Place your foot against the edge. Hold it!

Jack places his foot against the edge of the boat to hold onto the rod tightly and leans backward while reeling in his line.

Jack
What do you think? Tuna or sea bass? It must be at least twenty kilos. We'll have the best meal ever!

Jack starts to sing in celebration.

Waze3 chocolata w ta3mina waze3 chocolata w ta3mina.[8]

When he finally reels in his catch, he finds a huge stuffed animal in the shape of a fish attached to his line.

8 A popular Lebanese jingle "Give out chocolate and feed us!"

Jack stares at the catch in astonishment not yet able to understand what has just happened.

Nady, who orchestrated the whole prank, falls on the floor laughing. Jack realizes what Nady has done and starts hitting him while Nady laughs harder. Then Jack starts laughing as well.

Asshole! I swear you're such an asshole!

Nady
Ooohh God...I'm dying.

Jack
I swear, if you find a bigger jerk than yourself, you'll kill yourself! Come on, enough bullshit, let's move.

Nady gets up still laughing and goes to the helm. He tries to get the engine running but it doesn't start.

Cut to

Scene 37

Jihane's house at night

Jihane is watching TV. Sophia comes out of the kitchen and looks at Jihane for a moment. She contemplates her mother's loneliness.

Jihane
Something smells good! What's in the oven?

Sophia
Feta and wild thyme quiche. His favorite!

Jihane smiles, happy to hear that Sophia has prepared Jack's favorite dish.

Sophia
I'm going to take a shower and change.

Cut back

Nady is calling the coastguard for help, while Jack is sitting in the back of the boat feeling miserable.

Nady
Pan, pan, all ships, all ships. This is boat *Zefir* in position 1.5 nautical miles west of Ras Tabarja, lost my engine and drifting, require towing assistance. Boat *Zefir* over.

Jack
I thought you fixed this problem! Give me my phone. I have to tell them I'll be late. Damn, my bad luck!

Jack, in his misery, is staring at the floor, wondering how to break the news to Sophia. Nady, still talking to the coastguards, grabs Jack's phone and throws it to him. Jack, not paying attention, does not catch it and the phone falls in the sea.

The sound of the splash brings Jack back to reality.

Jack
Nady, I am in no mood for your pranks. I'm fed up with you!!

Nady
That was your phone!!

Jack
Nady, I'm serious, I could kill someone right now!

Nady rushes to where the phone sank and starts looking for it. He uses a flashlight.

Nady
That WAS your phone, I'm not kidding!

Jack finally realizes that Nady is serious and that it's not another one of his pranks. Jack grabs the small fishing net, kneels next to Nady, and starts trying to fish his phone out.

Jack
How many times have I told you not to throw the phone to me?!

Nady
YOU told me to throw it, but you weren't paying attention!

Jack
Liar! I didn't say throw it! I said hand it to me.

Jack, furious, pushes Nady to the floor and attempts to strangle him.

Scene 38
Jihane's house at night

Sophia who's dressed simply but elegantly is at the sink doing the dishes. Jihane is standing next to her drying them. They are working silently. The doorbell rings. Sophia shows no reaction. Jihane gets the door.

Jack, still in his beach outfit is holding a tiny gift bag.

Jack
I'm sorry! The boat's engine died while at sea.
And my phone fell in the water!

Jihane remains silent.

Jack
I know that you hate me.

Jihane
No, Jack, I don't hate you.
I just hate to see Sophia upset.

Jack
Can I talk to her?

Jihane
She's in the kitchen.

Jihane pauses.

You know Jack...it's really easy for a man to please a woman, if he chooses to do so.

Jack nods in appreciation and heads toward the kitchen.

Sophia intentionally focuses on doing the dishes despite the fact that Jack is standing behind her.

Jack
I'm not going to give excuses that you probably won't believe. But I want you to know this: There's no place I would have rather been tonight than here, having dinner with you.

He takes a step toward her and plants a kiss on the back of her head while she is still doing the dishes.

I am so sorry.

Jack pauses.

You know, recently someone told me that I am more interested in the sound of my own voice than in listening to what the person in front of me is trying to tell me. I believe he is right.

Sophia
When I was a little girl, I would wait every night for my father to come home. Every time I saw a plane, I felt sure he was on it. I watched how my mom did everything on her own and ended up alone.

Sophia takes a deep breath as if the weight of the world is on her chest.

I don't want to end up like her.

Jack
I'm sorry, I didn't notice all that.
I was too preoccupied with myself.

Jack takes out a small box from the gift bag, opens it, and places it on the kitchen table. Inside is a bracelet inlaid with small diamonds with "Love" etched on it. Jack leaves.

Scene 39
Jack's car

The next day, Jack is in his car at a red traffic light thinking about the night before. His phone beeps.
He receives a WhatsApp voice message.

It's from his boss, Nabil.

Nabil
Hi, Jack. Pass by my office. There's something I need to discuss with you.

Scene 40
Nabil's office

Jack arrives. He's excited and happy. He knocks and Nabil (45 years old) opens the door.

Nabil
Please have a seat.

Jack sits down.

Nabil
How are you?

Jack
Awesome

Jack jokingly smiles.

Don't you worry about anything.
Get on that plane and leave... and never come back.

Nabil
The decision has changed, Jack.

Jack
What decision?!

Nabil
The Head of Department.
The board picked someone else.

Jack
Someone else! Like whom?!

Nabil
Jean Provot

Jack
Jean! Are you kidding me?
Are you saying that Jean is more qualified than I am?!

Nabil
Jack, you know my opinion on this issue.

Jack
No, I don't. What I do know is that Jean doesn't have a quarter of the qualifications or the experience that I have. I bent backward, destroyed my marriage in the process, to finish that doctorate degree that you encouraged me to do. And now you tell me they want Jean to head the department!!

Nabil
The French own half of the hospital, Jack!

After a moment of silence, Jack gets up and takes off his white medical gown.

Nabil
What are you doing?!

Jack
I refuse to work under someone who is less qualified than I am!

Nabil
Jack, don't be irrational. You know that all the top positions in hospitals are taken!

Jack
I won't die of hunger. I have my private practice and I have a marriage in intensive care that I'm desperately trying to keep alive!

Jack leaves.

Nabil
Jack...Jack....

Scene 41

William's house

William is relaxing in a lounge chair, wearing a bathing suit, reading in the sun.

Mateo is lying down on a workout bench doing chest presses under a heavy bar of weights. Whenever he lifts the weights, he encourages himself by making a weird loud grunting noise as if it is coming from his gut.

Distracted, William looks at Mateo in disbelief.

William
Champ, what exactly are you training?
Your intestines?!

Mateo cracks up laughing and is unable to lift the bar again. He gets stuck under it.

William
Tsk tsk tsk! Tragic!

Mateo
William, please, not when I'm training.

William
You consider this training?!
Blindfolded, one would think you're throwing up!

Mateo laughs again and can't lift the bar off his chest. Jack arrives, puts his bag on the floor, and then helps Mateo lift the bar he's stuck under.

Mateo
He's crazy. He wants to kill me.

Jack sits on a chair next to William, clearly in a bad mood.

William
What's the matter? Always cranky!

Mateo
Who's Mr. Grumpy today!?

They laugh.

Jack
Am I amusing you both?!

William
What is it today?

Jack
Later

Jack notices the picture of the hammock that William uses as a bookmark. He takes a closer look at it. The hammock is hung between two trees insome woods. The scene looks inviting and relaxing.

Jack
How I wish I was at the far end of the world lying in one of those!

William
With Sophia holding you tight?

Jack looks at William without answering.

flashback

Scene 42
Miuca's cabin at sunset

*

The song "Color me In" by Damien Rice plays in the background.*

On a wide relaxing hammock hung between two evergreen trees in a lost wood adjacent to a charming cabin, William is lying with Miuca in his lap. Both of them are naked with only a light blanket covering them. William is playing with a lock of her hair. On Miuca's waist is a box of chocolate truffles. William takes one.

William
What's with the chocolate craving after sex?

Miuca
You lack affection, sweety.

William laughs and offers her a truffle. She refuses.

William
Are you saying no to me?!

Miuca
Uh-hah

William
Do you know what happened to the last woman who said no to this?

Miuca
What happened to her?

William
She didn't gain weight.

Miuca laughs.

William
I'm not going to stop tempting you until you have one.

William puts a chocolate truffle in his mouth and sucks on it pretending to be in a state of ecstasy. Miuca teasingly still refuses to indulge. William takes another truffle from the box and holds it between his thumb and index finger.

This is Earth. I'm lying right here.

William points to a spot on the truffle.

You are holding it between your two fingers. You have the power to do anything you want with it. You can even crush it if you want.

Miuca
Where did you say you were?

William
Right here.

William points again to the spot on the truffle. Passionately, she takes a bite of chocolate, nibbling William's finger in the process.

They kiss passionately.

Cut to

The song "Color me In" still in the background.

In the evening, Miuca and William are still lying in the hammock, under the light blanket. Opera music is playing softly.

The full moon and a few candles are enough to light up the scene.

William is reading out loud from a book while Miuca is listening to him.

Cut to

The next day, inside the cabin, Miuca's paintings are lying in every corner and hanging on every wall.

William is on the sofa, sitting still. He is posing with an old broomstick in his outstretched hand, perched sideways, wearing linen pants and a sky-blue unbuttoned shirt revealing one shoulder. Miuca, in an oversized white shirt, is standing in front of him, facing a canvas placed on an easel, painting something that William can't see.

William
I hope you will finish today, God willing!!

Miuca
Oh, it's looking perfect, babe!

William
I can't feel my arm! And what's with the broomstick?

Miuca
The broom is just for the pose, silly!
I'll replace it with something else later on.

Moments later.

William
Enough!

Miuca
Nooo! Don't get up!

William gets up, throws the old broom on the floor, and shakes his hand to get rid of the numbness.

William
Enough torture!

He heads over to the painting to see how it's coming out.

Miuca moves away toward the couch and starts laughing.

William looks at the painting and sees that it has nothing to do with him at all. It's a portrait of a girl's face which Miuca was copying from a passport photo that was attached to the top of the easel.

William
What's this? Where's my portrait?!

Miuca starts laughing and hides behind the sofa.

Miuca
In my heart.

William realizes that she's been playing with him all along and doesn't know whether to laugh or be angry.

William
I'm going to pull it out, this heart of yours!

William starts chasing her around the sofa. Miuca is laughing hard, while running away from him.

William
You have no idea what I'm going to do to you.

William picks up the broomstick and shakes it at her.

William
I'm going to brush your hair with this!

William begins to chase her again. Miuca runs to her palette and picks up her paintbrush threateningly.

Miuca
Come near me and I'll get you!

William tries to jump over the sofa to catch her but she swipes him with her paintbrush first, drawing a big "M" on his shirt and face. He looks in the mirror to see what she has done and goes ballistic.

She starts laughing and screaming, drops the paintbrush, and rushes to the garden throwing herself in the hammock.

Miuca
Sorry William!

William
What should I do with you now?

He kisses her for a few seconds while they lie across the hammock. Miuca laughs.

William
Wait.

William disappears for a couple of seconds and returns with a camera. He points it toward the hammock and sets the timer.

William
Do you know that we don't have a single picture together?! Other than the one in your heart, of course!

William runs to the hammock.

Move, move, move!

He throws himself on it. It flips over and they both fall on the ground screaming and laughing. The hammock swings empty.

The camera takes a picture of the empty hammock.

Flashback ends

Scene 43
Interior design office

Sophia enters her office to the pleasant surprise of a huge bouquet of red roses. As she admires the bouquet, she finds a card that reads: "I do not want to live without you" in Jack's handwriting.

Scene 44
William's house

William is exercising with Jack in the pool.
Next to them, Mateo is relaxing. William is holding the foam dumbbells, lifting them up.

Jack
Hold your elbows at ninety degrees.
Twist your wrists left, right, left, right.

Jack helps William to perform the exercise correctly.

Jack
Now sing "Frère Jacques..."

William throws a foam dumbbell at him and they laugh.

William
Finally, you communicated not quarreled.
She opened up to you! And you...
you're something else.
You're starting to crack her code.

Jack
I learned from the best.

William
But you have to move onward from here. Hit the steel
while it's hot. Think of something she loved to do
but you never did for her.

Jack

Jack pauses and looks like he's thinking hard.

Uff...picking out furniture together!

William
Oh, Why God WHY?! What have I done to deserve this?!
Jack, pick out furniture?!

Jack
Okay, okay, okay!!... Dancing. She loves to go dancing.

William
Thank you.
Find out where she is going out this weekend.

Jack
She's going to Effy's.

William is surprised by Jack's quick reply.

Jack
Mutual friends told me. They are going out together.

Mateo
But you really need to change your style.
A serious makeover!!

Jack
Why, what's wrong with my style?
You don't like the way I dress up?

William and Mateo glance at each other and break into laughter.

Jack
Jerks.

William
Know, if your woman is going there to dance,
you must lead her.

Jack
Lead her where?! Let's start with a civilized hello!

William
You just focus on the dancing and leave the rest to me.
But when I say lead her, I mean really lead her...
Pull her close in a way that she remembers your smell!

Jack
Remembers my smell?!

William
How good are you at dancing?

Jack
Great!

William
Why do my guts say otherwise?

He looks at Mateo, who nods his head in agreement.

William
Show us.

Jack
Piss off, guys.

William
Show us!

Jack
It's not rocket science! There!

He does a couple of clumsy dance moves.
William and Mateo look at each other and burst out laughing.
Jack, enraged, starts hitting them as they laugh even harder.

Jack
Screw you! I'm leaving!

Mateo stands in his way and grabs him firmly by the waist.
Jack reacts with shock.

Mateo
You hold her like this.

Jack tries to take a step backward out of Mateo's hold,
but William blocks his way grabbing him from behind by the waist.

Jack finds himself sandwiched between the two of them.

William
This is how you make her remember your smell.

Mateo
One, two, three, four ...one, two, three, four...

As the three of them do the dance steps over and over so Jack can learn, the housekeeper comes out onto the terrace.

When they notice her heading toward them, they split up in a comical way as if nothing was happening: Mateo looks up to the sky, Jack whistles and William gets in the water.

William goes underwater. At the far end of the pool, he once again sees the same two women that he previously saw. This time they are smiling at him and gesturing for him to come to them. William keeps looking at them until Jack pulls him out of the water.

Jack
Are you ok?!

William nods.

Scene 45
William's house at night, his room

William is on a video call with Jack, who is getting ready for the evening.

William
Change the shirt.

Jack
Why?!

William
You can't wear a polka-dotted shirt with a striped jacket! Wear something plain. On the double!

Jack
Okay, Okay!

Jack unbuttons his shirt.

But I feel weird showing up all by myself.

William
Just get to the bar and don't worry about the rest. What will you drink tonight?

Jack
I guess a beer...or a bloody mary!
William
God help me!! A red drink?!
Scotch, kiddo, a scotch with two ice cubes!

Scene 46
Night Club

Close up on an empty glass, two ice cubes are thrown in followed by some scotch. The bartender hands the drink to Jack who is seated at the bar. Jack takes a sip and makes a face at its taste.

A sexy woman in her forties, approaches the bar wearing a low-cut dress that shows her ample cleavage. Solange (45 years old) seductively slides up next to Jack and places one hand on his thigh.

Solange

Solange looks at the bartender.

Same for me, please.

Solange winks at Jack.

Hi, Hon

Jack
And you are?!

Solange
I'm the bait.

Jack
What bait?!

Solange
The one that goes on the hook of a fishing rod to catch the fish. I was told you like fishing.
Seems that William didn't tell you.

Jack
Tell me what?!

Solange
That I would come to spark the fire.
I'm here to make your wife want you again.

Jack
What wife! I want to spend the rest of my life with you and have at least seven kids.

Solange

Solange laughs.

You're a bit late, my love.

Sophia and her friends arrive and sit at their table. Sophia's friend suddenly nudges her with her elbow so hard that Sophia almost loses balance.

Sophia
What's gotten into you?!

Sophia's Friend
Check the bar! 9 o'clock! Do it subtly...

Sophia is dumbfounded to see Jack all dressed up with Solange at his side.
Their eyes meet. He raises his glass to her.

Cut to

The night has kicked off, the night club is packed... Sophia and her friends have clearly had a few rounds of drinks and shots.

Sophia
I can't believe the woman he's with! She's as old as his grandmother!

Sophia's Friend
Darling, all men are the same! When they're young they want a mature woman and at fifty they run after twenty-year-olds!

A waiter comes to Sophia's table with a bottle of pink Moet and champagne glasses.

At the bar, Solange places her hand on Jack's neck, who looks surprised.

Solange
Say something.

Jack
Like what?

Solange
Say anything. Just put three words together.

Jack
I don't get you!

Solange laughs dramatically and pretends to be enjoying herself tremendously. The waiter indicates to Sophia that the champagne bottle is from Jack. Sophia looks toward him only to witness the orchestrated scene between him and Solange.

Solange
Okay darling, it's time for me to go to the washroom and disappear down the drain.

Jack
Stay!

Solange

Solange pinches his cheek.

Darling, we want to ignite her fire, not defuse a bomb!

Solange takes her handbag and leaves.
At the same time, Jack's phone lights up.
It's a text message from William.

William
Try to be funny. And don't forget to compliment her.

At the right moment, Jack appears behind Sophia while she's dancing and places his hands on her waist. She gives in for a second, then tries to get out of his hold, but he pulls her back into his arms and she lets him.

Sophia
Leave me alone... go to your girlfriend.

Jack
Are you jealous?!

Sophia
Hehe, yes, very.

Jack
She's a patient. She came over to say hello.

Sophia
Ooh!! A patient! What position was she in to pull her neck muscle?

Jack
I've missed you.

He whispers in her ear, squeezing her body against his while moving to the music. Jack bends his head and breathes into her neck.

I missed your scent.

Sophia is tipsy. She tries to resist him in vain as her emotions fail her.

Sophia
You're an idiot.

Jack
And you're beautiful.

Eyes closed, she loses herself to him and the music.

Cut to

Scene 47

William's house

The room is dimly lit. William coughs repeatedly. His phone beeps. He checks it. It's a picture of Jack and Sophia dancing in each other's arms. He puts down the phone. William's coughing worsens. He begins to drown in his dark thoughts and appears worried and scared.

William
Talk to me... talk to me...

Enraged, he pushes everything off his bedside table onto the floor.

He opens the drawer next to him and takes out some morphine and a syringe. He fills the syringe from the vial.

He tightens the band around his arm and injects himself with the needle.

Cut back

Jack, boldly, turns Sophia to face him.

Jack
I don't want to live without you.

They stand there, looking into each other's eyes.

Cut to

Scene 48
Jack and Sofia's house

The door opens. Jack and Sophia are frantically removing each other's clothes while kissing. Jack's jeans get stuck around his ankles. They lose their balance and land on the couch.

The next morning, Sophia wakes up. It takes her a moment to realize where she is. Lying by her side, Jack smiles at her. He was watching her while she slept.

Jack
Good morning.

Sophia smiles back at him despite the thousand questions running through her head.

Great morning.

He kisses her lips.

Perfect morni...Coffee?

Sophia
Please.

Jack jumps out of bed and heads to the kitchen. Sophia is still processing what happened last night. Jack's phone is on the bedside table next to Sophia. It starts ringing.

Annoyed, she presses the silent button without really focusing on the caller ID. She does a double-take and looks at the phone. She blinks. It is William's profile picture.

Sophia
Hello...hello...

Nobody answers and the line cuts. At that moment, Jack returns with the coffee.

Jack
Who was it?

Sophia

Sophia begins to shake.

Why is William calling you?!

Jack
William is a patient of mine.

Sophia
A patient?!

Jack
He has cancer and I'm taking care of him.

Sophia
William has cancer?!

Jack
Yes. But where do YOU know him from?

Sophia is speechless.

Jack
Sophia?!

Scene 49
William's house

Jack rushes to William's house. He parks his car in the middle of the driveway, leaves the car door open, and rings the doorbell repeatedly. Then he urgently knocks on the door. The housekeeper opens the door and Jack furiously pushes past her. He finds Mateo.

Jack
Where is he?!

Jack rushes toward the bedroom. He enters it like a wild animal. Fatigued and fragile, William is in bed, coughing.
Jack grabs him by the shirt.

Jack
You jerk! Have you no morals?! You made me believe that you were my friend! Where did you sleep with her? On this bed? In the pool? Where I train you and take care of you!? Where?!!

Mateo enters the room, pulls Jack off of William and pushes Jack to the ground. William's cough worsens.

Mateo
Have you gone mad??

Jack attempts to get up but Mateo pins him down firmly by the neck, almost choking him.

Mateo
If you go near him again, I'll kill you.

Jack's face is red from Mateo's grip on his neck.

William
Leave him, Mateo, leave him!

Mateo
Calm down and act like a human being.

Jack, who is almost choking, nods his head in approval. Mateo lets him breathe once again and gives him some water.

Jack drinks.

William
Leave us.

Mateo
No way.

William
Mateo!

Mateo gives in and when leaving he turns toward Jack.

Mateo
I'll kill you if you lay a finger on him!

William
So, she spent the night at your place.

William is in bed, looking proud of himself.
Jack is still on the floor.

Jack
Is it entertaining for you to manipulate us like that?

William
Each one of us is played around with somehow!
Five months ago, I ruled the world.
I thought if I got you back together...

Jack
You should have told me!

William
Told you what?
"Hi Jack, I'm William. I slept with your wife."

Jack
You're a scumbag!

William
You were divorcing. It could have been anybody.

Jack
Still...you're a scumbag!

William
Okay... I'm a scumbag! But do you want to go on playing the role of the martyr or do you want to man up and discuss what's actually wrong?!
What got the two of you
to this point in your marriage?

Jack gives William the middle finger.

William
Bravo! That's what you're good at. Don't start crying now!
Is your lower lip trembling or am I mistaken?

Jack
There's a reason you're lying in this bed.
Do you know what it is? It's proof that God exists!

William
And God would have let you marry a woman
like Sophia?!

Jack
Don't you dare mention her name!

At this point, William starts looking up at the ceiling ignoring Jack's reactions as if to say: "You know what? Fuck this, you're not worth it."

Jack
At the end of your life, you're lying here in this bed all alone, like a cockroach. No family.
No Miuca... Where is she?! Tell me!
Or did she discover the real you?!

William doesn't answer. He just looks at Jack with insignificance.

Jack
I'll tell you why you're all alone: because you're a prick!

William
And do you want to know how big a prick I really am?!

flashback

Scene 50
Cyprus Hotel

Outside the hotel where William and Miuca first met, the mayor, Miuca dressed in white, her maid of honor and Dr. Fouad are all waiting on the sandy beach.

Miuca looks at Dr. Fouad as if she's asking him: "Where is he?!" Dr. Fouad shrugs his shoulders. William arrives singing. It's obvious he's been drinking.

He kisses Miuca.

Miuca
Have you been drinking?

William
Un poquito

Mayor
Okay. Let's do this.

Cut to

Two hours earlier

William is standing in front of the glass window of his hotel room, deep in thought. He's wearing off-white pants and a white shirt. A knock at the door breaks his train of thought.

William
Come in.

The room service guy enters with a jacket and hands it to William.

Room service
Your jacket, Sir.

William
Thank you.

The room service guy leaves. Facing a mirror, William puts on his jacket and then stares at himself.

Scene 51

Hotel Bar

William walks into the bar for a drink.

William
Tequila, please.

The bartender turns around.
It's the same guy from when he first met Miuca.

Bartender
Hey! Has tizi man!

William

William smiles.

Yeah. Has tizi big time.

The bartender pours him a tequila shot.
Facing William, two sexy ladies smile at him while checking him out. William raises the shot at them before gulping it down.

Cut back

Some of the mayor's speech is blurred out, but keywords about commitment remain. As if each word was hammering William's brain.

Mayor
"Your life will change"... "There is no more 'you' only 'us'"...
"Sacrifices, sacrifices, sacrifices"... "Forever, ever, ever"

Cut to

An hour earlier

William, the two sexy ladies and the bartender are drinking and laughing. The bartender starts pouring another round of tequila shots but William flips his glass upside down.

William
No, no, no!

Lady #1
Come on!

William
I have a wedding to attend.

Lady #2
Seriously?! Is that still legal?!

They laugh.

Lady #1
Come to our room. We have weed!

William
Ciao, ladies.

William walks to the bathroom and splashes his face with water. He looks into the mirror talking to himself.

William
I...I...Yes, you do! Yes, you do!
I...I...

Slaps himself once then twice. Pointing his finger and threatening himself.

William
YOU DO!!

Cut back

Mayor
Please, face each other, hold each other's hands, and repeat after me:

Miuca says her vows first and ends them with "I DO" but when it's William's turn, his voice starts to break bit by bit until it's his turn to say it, but nothing comes out.

Everyone is staring at him but he is just not there.

Suddenly, he comes back to the moment and looks into Miuca's eyes with so much love. He kisses her.

William
I love you so much!

William takes off, leaving everyone in shock.

Flashback ends

Scene 52
William's house

Jack looks at William with disgust.

William
Disgusted?!

Jack
What a prick you are!!!

William
Yeah right, because you earned the husband-of-the-year award for outstanding performance!

Jack
At least, I'm still with her.

William

William gives Jack a sarcastic look.

Yeah, you're welcome.

Jack
At least, I'm not a coward who flees when things get real.

Mateo knocks on the door and enters.

Mateo
William, your appointment is here.

William
Okay.

Mateo approaches to help him.
Leaving the room, William stops and turns toward Jack.

What has happened, happened.
A bit cruel, maybe.
Now, it's up to you to see the half-full part of the glass, or the half-empty one. Adios.

Cut to

William and Dr. Omar are on the terrace having breakfast.

Dr. Omar
I'm sorry I didn't visit you before.

But honestly, it aches me to see the William I know like this, being the man you are.

William
God bless you, doctor. No doubt the ministry is taking up all your time. I, too prefer you didn't see me in this state. Thank you for making it at such short notice.

Dr. Omar
Anything for you.

William
Very well then. You are aware of how much my company is worth.

Dr. Omar
Of course.

William
I own forty-five percent of it. I would like to donate my share to the Cancer Center that you founded.

William pauses.

Dr.Omar
That's very generous...

William
I have one wish.

Scene 53
Pub at night

Jack is broken, drunk and sitting alone at the bar. He finishes his drink in one gulp and leaves.

Lost and confused, Jack wanders the streets.

Scene 54
William's house

William is stretched out on his favorite couch, reading a book. The doorbell rings, and after a moment, the housekeeper appears.

Housekeeper
Sir, there's a lady at the door.

Sophia appears behind her.

Housekeeper
Ma'am!

William
It's ok.

The housekeeper leaves. William sits up. Sophia freezes, shocked to see him in such bad shape. He invites her to take a seat. She does. Heavy silence.

William
Late, as usual.

She barely smiles still contemplating his condition.

Sophia
Why did you do that?

William
Frankly, I've done so much that I'm not sure what you're referring to.

Sophia
Cutting me out! Ghosting me!

William
To avoid you looking at me this way.

Sophia, shaken, moves her eyes to the floor.

Sophia
Sorry...This is all so confusing. I'm furious at you, but at the same time, I'm unable to...

Sophia, close to tears, stops as her voice starts to break. William rubs her arm, soothingly.

William
I'm ok...

Sophia looks up at him again.

Sophia
Clearly!

William
Don't let my looks fool you. A sickness can be the cure for many ailments. How have you been?

Sophia
Hating your guts.

Sophia smiles.

William
I know...love comes in different forms.

At his response, Sophia shakes her head.
She thinks: "Same old William."

William
Are you with someone? Cause if you're available I might have someone for you. He can be a pain in the ass occasionally...frequently actually.

Sophia laughs.

But he's a great chap, someone to hold on to.

She smiles, nodding affirmatively.

Sophia
Life's not fair!

William
You and Jack are back together...
Everything happens for a reason.

Sophia gives him a long endearing look before hugging him warmly.

Scene 55
Piano Bar

Drunk, Jack enters a bar, and heads toward the bartender.

Bartender
What would you like to drink?

Jack
Do you have any yogurt?

Jack's phone starts to ring. It's Sophia, he puts it on silent mode.
He turns around and notices a pianist playing a grand piano.

Cut to

Jack lying down under the piano, eyes closed while the pianist continues to play.

Jack's mind races through memories with Sophia:

Sophia is listening to one of her favorite songs and starts to dance to the beat.
Sophia teasingly steps in between him and the TV while he's watching a game.
Sophia is cooking, and suddenly, the pan goes up in flames.
Sophia and Jack are fighting, she starts to cry and Jack hugs her.

Under the piano, Jack opens his eyes.

Scene 56

William's house, his bedroom

William is sleeping. He feels a presence.

William
Mateo?!

From behind the wall appears a hooded robe, like the one a Franciscan priest would wear, except there is no one inside it.

William
Who are you! What do you want?!

Hooded Robe
You called for me.

William
Why me?!

Hooded Robe
Why not you? Or do you believe the Earth doesn't revolve without you?!!

William
I believe you are being unjust. It's too early for me.

Hooded Robe
You think you are entitled to time. I AM TIME.

William is silent. The hooded robe begins to retract.

William
Don't go!

Hooded Robe
What else do you want to know?

William
I don't know.

Hooded Robe
William the Great is scared!

William
What's next?

The hooded robe disappears.

Hey! Where are you taking me?!

Scene 57
Jack and Sofia's house

Sophia is in bed asleep. The front door creaks open and shuts. Jack walks into the room, still fully dressed, snuggles in bed behind her and hugs her.

Scene 58
William's house

William is stretched out on his favorite couch, lost in his thoughts, with earphones in his ears.
Mateo is tanning while flipping through a magazine.

William
Can you make me a cup of coffee?

Mateo
Of course.

Mateo enters the house.

*

William ponders for a moment.
*The music "Channels and Winds" * composed by Philip Glass and Ravi Shankar starts playing.*

He then gets up, walks slowly toward the pool, and throws himself in the water.

Under the water, William sees his mother and sister at the other end of the pool. They smile at him. He gazes at them for a bit then swims toward them.

Mateo returns with the coffee. He is surprised not to find William on the couch.

He looks around and panics seeing him floating face down in the pool.

Mateo
No, No, No!

He jumps in the water, swims to William and lifts his head out of the water.

No, No, Please, No!!

Scene 59
Hospital

Jack runs up the hospital stairs three at a time. Mateo is in the hall, waiting and crying. He heads straight toward the Intensive Care Unit and enters without permission.

The nurse follows him objecting.

Nurse
Jack, you can't go in...

Jack doesn't listen to her and continues.

Nurse
Jack, please!!!

William is in critical condition. Dr. Fouad is by his side, holding his hand.

Jack
How is he?

Dr. Fouad shakes his head in dismay. A nurse appears.

Nurse
Doctor. We need you. There's an emergency.

Dr. Fouad
Call someone else.

Nurse
There's no one else. Dr. Simpson already left.

Dr. Fouad goes with her reluctantly. Jack approaches William and sits next to him. He holds his hand as he looks at him, words stuck in his throat.

William opens his eyes with effort and whispers.

William
Ela re.

Jack forces a smile. William feels a pang of pain. Jack caresses William's forehead with one hand, as he holds William's hand with his other.

He whispers in his ear.

Jack
You're not alone. I'm here, I'm here...

William is in a state between awareness and unconsciousness.

Jack
...You are in the garden, in the hammock and Miuca is next to you. You fell on the ground and you are both laughing...

Flashback

Scene 60
Miuca's cabin

Miuca's hand is in William's hair as they lie on the ground, facing each other after falling from the hammock in Miuca's garden.

Cut to

Jack is still next to William, whispering to him, while William's eyes are open as if he can see the white tunnel.

Cut back

William hugs Miuca from behind, he smells and kisses her neck, while she has her arms stretched behind her wrapped around his waist, gripping his shirt with both hands. He is unbuttoning Miuca's oversized white shirt; they are kissing passionately.

Cut back

William's eyes are open, void of life.
Jack looks down at him, his eyes filled with tears.

Scene 61

Cancer Center, Dr Omar's office

Jack is seated and waiting. The secretary is working on her computer.

Jack
Excuse me, Ma'am, do you have any idea what this is about?

The secretary shakes her head. The office phone rings. She picks up, talks softly, and then hangs up.

Secretary
Please come in, His Excellency is waiting for you.

Jack
Thank you.

Jack enters the office. Dr. Omar is seated behind his desk, flipping through some papers in a file. He gets up to shake Jack's hand.

Jack
Good morning, Mr. Minister. You asked to see me?

Dr. Omar
Yes, please, have a seat.

Jack sits across from him.

Dr. Omar
You have quite an impressive file. Diplomas, a doctorate degree...And such a vast experience at your age! Congratulations.

Jack

Jack looks surprised.

Thank you.

Dr. Omar
We are searching for someone to head the Physiotherapy Department. And we would like that person to be you.

Dumbfounded, Jack tries to speak but he can't find his voice. Finally, he clears his throat and gains his voice again.

Jack
I am honored, Mr. Minister. Thank you.
But may I ask how you found me?

Dr. Omar
A mutual friend

Jack
A friend?!

Dr. Omar
Do you believe in angels?

Scene 62
William's house

Jack and Dr. Fouad are sitting facing each other.

Jack
How come I have never heard of or met any of his family members?

Dr. Fouad
His dad passed away when he was young.
Then he lost his mom and sister one after the other.
They were his soft spot.

Jack
Oh!!

Mateo enters carrying a box and hands it to Jack. Jack looks at him bewildered.

Mateo
William left it with your name on it.

Dr. Fouad's phone rings and he walks into the living room.

Cut to

Sitting on the bed in William's room, Jack stares at the box that Mateo gave him. After a few moments, he opens it. Inside is a vinyl record with a Brazilian singer on the cover, Miuca.

Jack
Miuca!!

Jack, confused, flips over the record. Sets it aside then goes back to the box.

At the bottom is the picture of the empty hammock that William used as a bookmark. Jack turns it over and notices the following words on its back:

"To the best brother ever. From Cyprus with love.
Miss you superstar, Janine"

*

Jack takes the vinyl record out of its sleeve and plays it on the turntable. The song "Você vai ver" by brazilian singer called Miucha, resonates around the room.*

He remembers when he had heard it before in this exact same room.

Jack rushes out of the room to find Dr. Fouad. In the living room, Dr Fouad is talking to Mateo.

Dr. Fouad
...Keep an eye on the house until I return from my trip.

Jack comes in like a madman.

Jack
Dr. Fouad!

Dr. Fouad is surprised at the urgency in Jack's voice.

Please Dr. Fouad, tell me you know Miuca!!

Dr. Fouad
Miuci! Who is Miuci?!

Jack
Miuca, Miuca, the woman William was in love with!

Dr. Fouad
Never heard of her! Miuca?! Does such a name exist?!

Jack
Yes! William was going to marry her in Cyprus,
and he deserted her at the altar! You were the best man!

Dr. Fouad
Me?!! What were you smoking in the other room?!

Jack drops onto the couch, immersed in his thoughts, trying to process the brutal truth, the fact that William is still manipulating him even after his death.

Cut to

six months later

Scene 63
William's grave

Jack and Sophia, who is visibly pregnant, are at William's grave. Sophia places a bouquet of flowers near the headstone. She looks at it with obvious gratitude in her eyes. Then, she turns to Jack.

Sophia

Sophia moves her hand to her belly.

William and I will be waiting for you in the car.

She softly caresses Jack's cheek. He warmly puts his hand on her belly above hers. She leaves the graveyard.

Jack blows the dust off the floor and then wipes it with his hand before sitting on the edge of the grave.

Jack
Ela re, my friend, how are we today?
From now on, we will change our routine,
I will talk and you will listen.

Jack laughs softly to himself.

Yesterday was Sophia and I's third wedding anniversary, And let me tell you, the surprise I planned was something else. Even you wouldn't have come up with that one.

Jack smiles jokingly, yet proudly.

It's true that the student eventually outdoes the teacher.

Jack laughs again.

I can imagine what you would have said if you were here. I miss you...
It's been a while since anyone told me off.
Every time I see a cup of yogurt, I laugh to myself like an idiot

Jack takes a shot-bottle of cognac and a cigarillo out of his pocket. He lights the cigarillo.

Jack
I'm sure you can smell this.

Jack raises his shot.

Cheers, my friend. There are very few who give you so much in life that they never leave...

Jack takes the picture of the empty hammock out of his pocket. He looks at it closely and places it against the headstone. Miuca's song "Voce vai ver" plays in the background.

The camera zooms in on the photo while a light breeze makes the fallen leaves on the ground twirl around it.

As the photo fills the frame, the hammock starts to swing slightly with the breeze while the sound of William and Miuca's laughter resonates.

Fade Out

In loving memory of Matilde and Janine

Where to, hereafter?

The oldest question in human history.
Fortunate are those with infinite faith—for them, the matter is settled. They know.

... While I'm at it, "infinite faith," not to say a blind one, includes both those who are certain of eternal life and those who are equally certain there's nothing beyond.

At school, we were taught Descartes' famous line:
"I think, therefore I am."
Cogito, ergo sum.

But the full version is often overlooked:
"I doubt, therefore I think, therefore I am."
Dubito, ergo cogito, ergo sum.

A certainty, linguistically speaking, is factual knowledge that allows no room for doubt—like saying the Earth is oval and revolves around the sun.

Faith, on the other hand, is a choice to believe. Like those who once believed the Earth was flat and the sun revolved around it—so fiercely that they stoned to death anyone who preached certainty.

Uff, enough! Here I go overanalyzing again.

Let's return to the age-old question:

What's beyond? (Tick the right answer)

a. Heaven

b. Hell

c. Reincarnation

d. Nothingness

The point is—it takes humility. No one holds the ultimate truth.

"Immortality" can be very simple. It's in how we live, in our deeds and their ripples, in the legacy we leave in this world... a world we inherited as a paradise—and have slowly turned into a living hell.

And perhaps the only certain truth is this:

We live on in the hearts and minds of those we have come across, spent time with, given to, and taken from.

In the memories they carry of us in their hearts, the smile or frown our memory paints on their faces... every time we cross their minds.

"Ela re," my friend.

Text
Abboudy Mallah

English translation
Mirna Karam and Abboudy Mallah

English copyediting and proofreading
Zeina Assaf

Arabic proofreading
Mohamed Hamdan

Graphic design
-scope Ateliers

Cover illustration
Laure Ibrahim

Published by
KAPH
ART BOOKS FROM THE ARAB WORLD
كتب الفن من العالم العربي

Beirut / Dubai
www.kaphbooks.com

ISBN: 978-614-8035-79-1

First edition, 2025

MIX
Paper | Supporting responsible forestry
FSC FSC® C163211

Papers used in this publication are FSC® certified, sourced from responsibly managed forests, recycled materials, and/or controlled sources.

Printed in July 2025
by Editoriale Bortolazzi-Stei, Verona, Italy.
Legal deposit August 2025.

Distribution in Europe
Les Presses du Réel
35 rue Colson
21000 Dijon
France
www.lespressesdureel.com

Idea Books
Nieuwe Hemweg 6R
1013 BG Amsterdam
The Netherlands
www.ideabooks.nl

Distribution in the Middle-East
CIEL Book Distribution
3rd Interchange, Al Quoz Industrial I
P.O.Box 282005
Dubai, UAE
www.ciel.me

MuseumShops Company / HAAL
Prince Turki Ibn Abdulaziz Al Awwal Rd,
Al Mohammadiyyah,
Dooryard 1st floor
Riyadh, KSA

Distribution in the Americas, Asia and Australia
ARTBOOK | D.A.P.75
Broad Street,
Suite 630
New York, NY 10004
www.artbook.com

1

Puppeteer

The Puppeteer

FADE IN

Maïn Characters

- William:

Middle aged, wealthy, self made, ~~educated~~ cultivated, ~~cocky~~ a small dose of God complex, fit, ~~boxing~~, swimming, reading, ~~bachelor~~, eternal bachelor, womanizer, kind, elegant

- outer conflict: illness, winning Sophia back from death bed, ~~staying in control~~ still got it Play defy Go
- inner conflict: scared of the unknown, loosing grip on destiny, ~~and~~ loneliness, questioning his life choic

- Jack:

~~F~~ 35 yrs old, middle class, self made, physiotherapist, ambitious, hardworking, married, struggling with his marrige, ~~cliche~~ typical middle eastern mindset, ~~average~~ "brouillon", ambitious

- outer conflict: winn's wife back, ~~make a point~~ ~~advance in~~ achieve more at work get to the t
- inner conflict: ~~stuck with~~ getting over his cliché relationship believes?? being able to ~~understand~~ forgive William

- Sophia:

30 yrs old, middle class, ~~married~~ unhappily married to Jack, self made, architect, pretty, elegant, ~~baby issues~~ miscarriage.

- outer conflict: Relationship with Jack - baby issues, how women imagine marriage ~~life as~~ versus reality
- inner conflict: Father figure issues - ~~lonely~~ ending up like her mother, ~~failed~~ marriages men run away from ~~wife~~ wives

Miucha
~~- Elia:~~

30's, William's lost love, painter ~~artist~~, half brazilian - half lebanese, (Metisse), pretty, ~~fanta~~ unconventional, cultivated, a free spirit,

- outer conflict: being ~~be~~ with William. they will meet on the beach in a meet cute ...
- inner conflict: ~~being~~ being with William!!! She's a fantasy, a dream

ACT I

- A disfunctional couple: ~~husband~~ Jack sleeping on the couch, ~~wife~~ Sophia sleeping in bed.

- William inside an MRI machine. All white reflecting on White tunnel that people with near death experiences talk about.

- Sophia ~~[illegible]~~ moves out of the house.

Insert boat scenes: fishing with friends

- Encounter between William and Sophia.

- Jack trying to ~~go~~ win Sophia back. She rejects him.

Insert Pool scenes for William

- Sophia is drawned into arrogant William's impressive lifestyle.

- Sophia finally succumbs to William's ~~[illegible]~~ charm: they sleep together

Leave the audience in doubt. Questioning if it happened or not.

* Sophia has baby issues

- 4 months Later William's ~~health drastic…~~ much thinner, p… half the man… Refuses treatment.

- Doctor suggests physio…

- William asks for So…

- The relation between … of them will start on … and it gets better w… session as William w… coach Him on getting hi…

- ~~Same time William wi… his long lost love~~ * Jack … prom…

- Jack goes to see Soph… and ask her for help … set a ~~meeting~~ dinner … him and Sophia.

~~(Flashbacks)~~

* William in the pool will see ~~[illegible]~~ Ghosts … (vision…

P.P 1

William is diagnosed with stage 4 cancer

it's sad, so sad, it's a sad sad situation

ACT II

لا تبكي يا
حبيب العمر

ACT III

*Sophia who haven't heard from William, since he vanished, must doubt his presence

P

to be emotionally and physically

- William will start telling his story about Zilia, his long lost true love.

~~root~~ in flashbacks. no story telling. everything happens on ~~screeen~~ screen.

- Jack's education on relationships continues.
- ~~As he~~ He knows where Sophia will party.
- William and Mateo decide to give Jack a different look.
- Mateo takes him to his barber and shopping for a complete make over (with his gay friends)

phia acept give ~~him a~~ another shot.

- Jack winning Sophia back at the party. They sleep together.

P.P 2
Jack discovers that William had an affair with Sophia!!

Mircha
brazilian singer

- Harsh confrontation between enraged Jack and tiered William.
- final flashback on how William screwed up with Zelia in a lunch & with friends ~~stan~~ He leaves her at altar
- ~~Zelia leaves him~~ drunk and wasted
- ~~Confrontation William and Sophia~~
- ~~William Angel death vs.~~
- Conversation between Angel of death, visits William at night
- William rushed to hospital
- ~~Jack goes to see Zelia and talks her into visiting him. She refuses as she is married.~~
- William in his last moments
- Jack with him is surprised with Zelia's visit. Zelia is a fantasy
- He dies in her arms.
- Jack's visit to William's ~~cemit~~ cemitery.

Jack will discover that still playing him even after death

آدم وحوّا كان مسموحلن كل شي "إلّا" التفاحة"،
وما تحملوا غيرها. معتّر اللي ملبوص كل حياته
بتفاحة"، وهو عايش بجاط فواكه! 

Ufff شو ~~بحا~~ بحلّل !!

يمكن ما ~~شافها هيك~~ أد ما بحلل ما عرفت إثبت.
بقولوا الأعزب بعيش ملك وبموت متل الكلب،
والمجوّز بيركض متل الكلب بس بموت ~~محلوظ~~ ملك.
بالآخر كلنا رح نموت. فأنا عايش ملك.
بس لمّا موت تصير وين بروح؟

③

جهنم؟ لا لا، أكيد لأ، عندي حساسية عالهبّ، بكره الشوب.
الجنة؟... ليوصل عليا الواحد بدّو يعيش بلا ~~كل~~
حياته بلا الإشيا للي "بسمّوها" خطايا... بشرّفق.
~~بجنّن~~ شي بجنّن!

وليام (٤٧ سنة، حفور لافش) مسطّح داخل ال IRM،
إضاءة ال IRM البيضاء من حوله.
فجأة بسمة ~~خفيفة~~ صغيرة مثالة على وجهه. 

وليام (٧.٥) (~~الحـ~~ الحديث براسه)

OK، بروح مطرح ما يكونوا النسوان الحلوين.

Dubai, April 9, 2019

APRIL 2019

~~Sooner or later~~ The Puppeteer

White is everywhere

داخل مكنة IRM

صوت تخطيط الـ IRM كأنما تأتي من بعيد، ~~لا نستطيع~~ دون

أن نميّز فعلاً ما هي.

ويليام (voice over)

كل اللي ~~وصلوا~~ شافوا الموت بخبروا إنن فاتوا بـ ~~Tunnel~~ نفق

أبيض طويل قبل ما يرجعوا ~~يعيشوا~~ عالحياة...

بآخر هال Tunnel شو في؟ ما حدا شاف!

هالدني ماشية لوحدا أو في حدا عم يحرّك الخيطان من فوق؟!

لما تعرف إنو الكرة الأرضية منّا إلّا نقطة غبرة بهالكون،

~~وتفكّر~~ أديش وتحسب أديش بدّو خيطات (long whistle)!!

~~لذيذ الطاحو يلعب~~

حلو اللعب بالناس، تخلقن رجّال أو مرا، بشع أو حلو،

غني أو فقير، Trisomique أو عادي،

مزوّج أو أعزب... Oops، آخر وحدي مش هو بقرّرا.

②

هو خلق آدم وحوّا. بس الله يلعن أبو هالتفاحة

~~شو~~ [illegible] ~~دفعنا حقا غالي~~ شو كلّفت غالي.

بعدنا لليوم عم ندفع حقّا.

معقول ~~طيب~~ أنا آكل سندويش دجاج ~~وثوم~~ اليوم،

وابن إبن إبنو لإبني يخلق عم يترشا ثوم!! HeHe

خلق آدم وحوّا وبعدين صاروا آدم وآدم، حوّا وحوّا.

بس كمان من ~~كتير~~ أد ما فشلنا بعلاقاتنا ما بقا عم

نعرف شو بدنا نعمل.

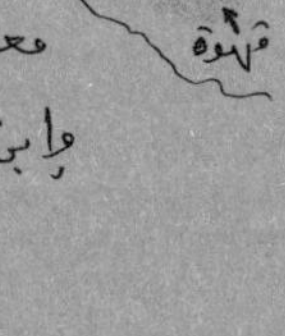

The puppeteer

محرّك الدمى

ملعّب الدمى

~~محرّك~~ الخيوط

سيّد المصير

~~دمى مشتركة~~

خيوط القدر

~~ماريونيتيست~~

BOFFF!!!

كعبث

Pierre Bachelet : Marionnettiste

مسيّرين أم مخيّرين ؟؟؟؟

~~[illegible]~~ Min Al? Ana Al

سيّد الدمى

محرّك الدمى

جواب ثنائي

نصّ
عبودي ملاح

الترجمة إلى الإنجليزي
ميرنا كرم وعبودي ملاح

التحرير اللغوي والتدقيق بالإنجليزية
زينة عساف

التدقيق اللغوي بالعربية
محمد حمدان

تصميم الكتاب
-سكوب أتيلييه

رسم الغلاف
لور ابراهيم

الناشر
KAPH
ART BOOKS FROM THE ARAB WORLD
كتب الفن من العالم العربي

بيروت / دبي
www.kaphbooks.com

الرقم التسلسلي:
978-614-8035-79-1

الطبعة الأولى، 2025

MIX
Paper | Supporting responsible forestry
FSC FSC® C163211

الأوراق المستخدمة في هذا المنشور حاصلة على شهادة FSC®، ومصنوعة من مصادر مدارة بشكل مسؤول، أو من مواد معاد تدويرها، و/أو من مصادر خاضعة للرقابة.

طبع في فيرونا، إيطالي
Editoriale Bortolazzi-Stei
الإيداع القانوني: أغسطس 2025

التوزيع الأمريكيتان – آسيا – أستراليا
آرتبوك | دي. آيه. بي 75 برودستريت،
جناح 630 نيويورك، 10004
www.artbook.com

فرنسا – سويسرا – بلجيكا – لوكسمبورغ
لو بريس دو رييل
35 شارع كولسون
21000، ديجون،
فرنسا
www.lespressesdureel.com

باقي أوروبا
أيديا بوكس
نيو هيوينغراخت 1013،
أمستردام، هولندا
www.ideabooks.nl

الشرق الأوسط
دار سيل للتوزيع التقاطع الثالث-
القوز- المنطقة الصناعية 1، صندوق
بريد 282005، دبي، الامارات العربية
المتحدة www.ciel.me

شركة متاجر المتاحف / طريق الأمير
تركي بن عبدالعزيز الأول المحمدية،
الدور الأول، مجمع دوريارد الرياض،
المملكة العربية السعودية

بعد هون لوين؟

أعتق سؤال بتاريخ البشرية!
نيّال الإيمانه مطلق، الأمور محسومة عنده، بيعرف كل شي!

و عا فوقا، الإيمان المطلق، لما قول أعمى، ما بيقتصر على الأكيدين من وجود حياة بعد الموت، بل بيشمل كمان المُصِرّين على عدم وجودها.

من نحنا و بالمدرسة علّمونا ديكارت:
" أنا أفكّر، إذن أنا موجود"
Cogito, ergo sum

بس الحقيقة إنه هيدي الجملة "اجتزأوها". جملة ديكارت الكاملة بتقول:
" أنا أشك، إذن أنا أفكّر، إذن أنا موجود"
Dubito, ergo cogito, ergo sum

أليقين، لغويا، هو العلم الذي لا يقبل الشك، مثل إنّك تقول إنه الأرض بيضاوية و بتدور حول الشمس.

أمّا الإيمان، فمعناه هو التصديق، و الناس كانوا مؤمنين بإنه الأرض مسطّحة، وإنه الشمس هي اللي بتدور من حولها، مؤمنين لدرجة إنهم رجموا حتى الموت كل مين بشّر آنذاك باليقين!

رجعت حلّل. أوف شو بحلّل!

طيّب تا نرجع للسؤال الأزلي:

بعد هون لوين ؟! (ضع إشارة جنب الإجابة الصحيحة)

أ. الجنّة.

ب. النار.

ج. التقمّص بكائن آخر.

د. العدم.

كل القصّة بتنحل بشويّة تواضع. ما حدا عنده الحقيقة المطلقة.

الخُلود في يكون شغلة كتير بسيطة. بطريقة عيشنا، الاشياء اللي منعمِلا و تردّداتا بهالكون، إرثنا بهالأرض... أرض ورثناها جَنّة و عم نحوّلا كل يوم أكثر و أكثر لجحيم.

و يمكن الحقيقة الوحيدة الأكيدة،

هي إنّا مِنضَل عايشين بقلوب و عقول الناس للي التقينا فيا، عاشرناها، اعطيناها و أخدنا مِنّا.

الذكريات للي بتحملا بقلبا عنّا، و البسمة أو العبسة للي رح تنرسم عا وجوها ... كل ما مرقنا بعقولها.

"Ela re," my friend.

يُقال إن النهر يرتجف من الخوف قبل دخوله إلى البحر.

ينظر إلى الوراء نحو الطريق الذي قطعه،
من قمم الجبال، والطريق الطويل المتعرج
الذي عبر الغابات والقرى.

وأمامه، يرى محيطاً شاسعاً،
لدرجة أن الدخول فيه يبدو وكأنه اختفاء إلى الأبد.

ولكن ليس هناك طريق آخر،
والنهر لا يستطيع العودة إلى الخلف.
لا أحد يستطيع العودة إلى الخلف.
فالعودة إلى الخلف مستحيلة فى الوجود.

النهر يحتاج إلى المخاطرة بدخول البحر
لأن عندها فقط سيختفي الخوف.
لأن هناك سيعرف النهر
أن الأمر ليس حول الاختفاء في البحر،
بل أن يصبح هو البحر

"The River"

– منسوب إلى جبران خليل جبران

fade in

المشهد ١

كل شيء لونه أبيض.

يُسمَع في الخلفية رنين متقطع لجهاز طبّي.

(صوت رجل / *voice over*)

اللي شافوا الموت بقولوا إنو فاتوا بنفق أبيض طويل
قبل ما يرجعوا للحياة...بآخر هالنفق شو في؟
ما حدا شاف! نحنا فعلاً مخيّرين أو في حدا عم
بِحَرّك الخيطان؟!
لمّا تستوعب إنّو كوكب الأرض وكل شي فيه مَتُن إلّا
نقطة غبرة بهالكون، قديش بدّا خيطان!! (صَفرة طويلة)

منخلق بأميركا أو قندهار، كروموزوم x أو y غني أو
فقير، مع داون سيندروم أو عادي، مزوّج أو أعزب.
أه، لأ آخر وحدي نحنا اللي منجني عحالنا فيا.
خلقنا آدم وحوا. وبعدين صرنا آدم وآدم، حوا وحوا.
بس كمان قد ما فشِلنا بِعلاقاتنا ما عم نعرِف بقا
شو بدنا نعمل.

أوف شو بحَلِّل!! يمكن قد ما بحَلِّل ما عرفت اثبت.
بِقولوا الأعزب بِعيش مَلِك وبموت متل الكلب،
والمجوّز بيركُض متل الكلب بس بِموت مَلِك.
بالآخر، كلنا رح نموت. فأنا عايش مَلِك.

بس لمّا تصير وين بروح؟
جهنّم؟ لا لا، أكيد لأ، عندي حساسية عالحرارة،
بكره الشوب.

الجنة؟... بستاهلا؟! التفاحة فاكهتي المفضلة!
بس عا سجلّي العدلي مكتوب «لا حُكم عليه»!
شي بيحيّر!

ويليام (٥٢ عاماً)، داخل جهاز التصوير بالرنين المغناطيسي، محاطاً بضوء أبيض.

فجأة، ترتسم على وجهه ابتسامة صغيرة ومحتالة.

أوك... بروح مطرح ما بكونوا النسوان الحلوين.

عبودي ملّاح

سيّدُ الدُّمى

KAPH

تم تعديل هذا النص من نسخته الأصلية كسيناريو سينمائي.
وأُعيد تنسيقه وصياغته ليناسب هذا الكتاب.

الشخصيات

ويليام
٥٢ سنة
رجل أعمال ناجح

صوفيا
٣٢ سنة
مصممة داخلية، زوجة جاك

جاك
٣٥ سنة
معالج فيزيائي، زوج صوفيا

ربيع
٣٥ سنة
طبيب نسائي، صديق جاك

ندي
٣٥ سنة
رائد أعمال، صديق جاك

جيهان
٦٠ سنة
والدة صوفيا

راجين
ناطور المبنى الذي تسكنه جيهان

طوني
مدير ويليام التجاري

جمال
شريك وعضو مجلس إدارة في شركة ويليام

سليم
شريك وعضو مجلس إدارة في شركة ويليام

د. عمر
مؤسس مركز سرطان الأطفال
صديق ويليام

د. فؤاد
٥٠ سنة
طبيب ويليام وصديق طفولته

ماتيو
٣٠ سنة
ممرّض ويليام

ميوتشا
٣٢ سنة
فنانّة، حبيبة ويليام

نبيل
٤٥ سنة
رئيس قسم العلاج الفيزيائي ومدير جاك

صولانج
٤٥ سنة
إمرأة مثيرة في ملهى ليلي

المشهد ٢
منزل جاك وصوفيا، ليلاً

موسيقى هادئة تملأ أجواء البيت. في غرفة النوم شموع مضاءة وبتلات من الورد الأحمر المنثورة على شراشف السرير البيضاء وعلى الأرض.
صوفيا (٣٢ عاماً)، ترتدي لباساً داخلياً رقيقاً مثيراً وتحمل في يدها كأساً من الشمبانيا، تجلس على حافة حوض الاستحمام وتتفقد درجة مياه حمّام الفقّاعات المزيّن ببتلات الورد العائمة.

على طاولة صغيرة، توجد زجاجة شمبانيا موضوعة في دلوٍ من الثلج وكأس فارغ، وبجانبها طبق من الجبن وورقة صغيرة كتب عليها بخط اليد: "Happy second wedding anniversary my love"

المشهد ٣
مدخل مستشفى، ليلاً

جاك (٣٥ عاماً)، يخرج مستعجلاً من المستشفى حاملاً حقيبته ويصعد إلى جانب ربيع في jeep رباعي الدفع

ربيع
وينك يا أخي؟ شو بطّل في معالج فيزيائي غيرك ببيروت؟!

ربيع ينطلق بسيارته بينما جاك يرسل من هاتفه رسالة نصّية عبر تطبيق واتساب.

المشهد ٤
منزل جاك وصوفيا

صوفيا تشعل البخور وتستمتع برائحته الطيبة.تتلقى رسالة عبر تطبيق واتساب، تقرأها، ثم تضع هاتفها جانباً. تصفن للحظة قبل أن تطفئ الشموع الموضوعة أمامها.

Cut to

المشهد ٥
قارب صيد، ليلاً

قارب صيد راسٍ في قلب البحر. جاك وربيع وندي (٣٥ عاماً) وقد ألقوا صنارات الصيد، يشربون البيرة ويتحدثون.

جاك

... ليك حبيبي، شئت أم أبيت من الـ٢٠٠٠ لهلّق الفرنساويي مسيطرين عالفوتبول.آخر ٧ كاس العالم عاملين أربعة فينال، ربحانين اثنينن وخسرانين اثنينن بالـpenalties يعني منّا حتى خسارة شرعية!

ندي

حياتي إنت وفريق الـ «blondies» تبعك،
لازِم تِرفعوا علم الزائير.

ندي يتجه نحو صندوق التبريد، يتناول منه زجاجتي بيرة، ويرمي واحدة لكل من ربيع وجاك.
جاك يرمق ربيع بنظرة تقول «معقول شو عم يحكي هيدا؟!»

جاك

(مخاطباً ربيع)

پليز فسّرلو لهيدا الأمّي إنّو صار إسمه الكونغو.
بعدين كلّه صار هيك! شو فريق الألمان عِرق آري يعني؟! خضيرة وأوزيل وخان. هودي لعّيبة خلقوا وربيوا بهالبلدان، خلص.
وسّعلي عقلك العنصري شي شوي!

ندي

بدي وسّعلك غير شي أنا.

جاك

ناوِلني هالتلفون حاج تكتِّر حكي.

ندي يتناول هاتفاً من صندوق بجوار مقعد القبطان حيث يضع الجميع هواتفهم، ويلقي به إلى جاك.
جاك يتعثر قليلاً قبل أن يلتقطه.

جاك

صرت قايِلّك مية مرّة ما تكِبّو هيك. بركي وقع بالماء!

ندي

بتسقطه بالرزّ، بيسحب الرطوبة منّه.

ندي يقف عند حافة القارب، ويتبوّل في البحر.

ربيع

بشرفك ولو!!!!

ندي
لازم فضّي لإرجع عبّي. Empty full, empty full!

ربيع
طيّب روح لتاني ميل.

ندي
مشوار.

جاك ينظر إلى هاتفه مستغرباً. صوفيا قرأت رسائله على واتساب لكنها لم تجبه بعد.

ربيع
في شي؟

جاك
صوفيا، ما عم تجاوبني.

ندي
نيّالك، يا ريت مرتي كمان بتبطِّل تجاوبني.

ربيع
شو الوضع هالإيام؟

جاك
خرا.

ربيع يضحك.

جاك
سامِع بالرمال المتحرّكة؟ إيه نحنا بالخرا المتحرّك.

ربيع
بعد ما شفت شي! نطور ليجي الولد.

ندي ينتهي من التبول ويعود إلى مكانه. يمسك خد جاك ويقرصه.

ندي
(ممازحاً)

إنتِ بدِّك تبذّري يا صغيرة؟

جاك

يُبعد يد ندي عن خدّه.

شيل إيدك عنّي يا مقرف!

ربيع
ما تنسوا هيدا السبت عيد ميلاد إبني «تيمي»

جاك
مان sorry ما رح إقدر، السبت عم روح على صفوف الدكتوراه. «تيمي» مش خلقان بـ ٢٨؟

ربيع
والسبت بيكون ٢٨.

جاك محللاً للحظة قبل أن يدرك شيئاً ما...

جاك
السبت ٢٨، يعني بكرا ٢٧، يعني اليوم ٢٦!!

جاك يبدو وكأنه رأى شبحاً للتو. يضرب جبينه بيده ويبدأ في الركض في أرجاء القارب، ويجمع صنارات الصيد على عجل.

جاك
اليوم ٢٦!!

ربيع
شو في؟! شو صار؟!

ندي
واضح ما بيحب الـ ٢٦.

يقف جاك على حافة القارب.

جاك
اليوم عيد زواجي!!

ربيع
أووو! طيّب طيّب روق.

في لحظة يأس، يدع جاك جسده يسقط من حافة القارب إلى مياه البحر.

المشهد ٦
منزل جاك وصوفيا

يُفتح الباب الرئيسي للمنزل. يدخل جاك وهو لا يزال مبللاً بالماء، ويضع أغراضه على الطاولة. تشير الساعة المعلقة على الحائط إلى الواحدة ليلاً. يرى طاولة غرفة الطعام قد جُهِّزَت لعشاء رومانسي لشخصين.
يدخل إلى غرفة النوم الغارقة في الظلام دون أن يُشعل الضوء، ظناً منه أن صوفيا نائمة.

يتوجه إلى الحمام بهدوء، يشعل الضوء، فيتفاجأ ببتلات الورد والشموع وكاسات الشمبانيا وحوض الاستحمام الممتلئ بالماء.
يعود إلى الغرفة باتجاه السرير ليتفاجأ بأن صوفيا ليست هناك.
يشعل الضوء، ويرى المزيد من بتلات الورد المنثورة على الأرض وعلى السرير. يتجه نظره نحو خزانة الملابس. يرى بابها مفتوحاً وقد أفرغت من الثياب. يتفقّد طاولة منضدة الزينة والتبرّج الخاصة بصوفيا، فيجدها فارغة تماماً هي أيضاً.

في تلك اللحظة، يدرك جاك أن صوفيا قد جمعت أغراضها وغادرت المنزل. يُطلقُ تنهيدةً طويلة، يغمض عينيه يائساً. يُلقي بثقله على السرير ويظلّ مستلقياً هناك للحظة، محدّقاً في السقف.

وأخيراً، يمسك جاك هاتفه ويتّصل بصوفيا.

عاملة الهاتف
«إن الرقم المطلوب غير متوفر حالياً، نرجو المحاولة لاحقاً».

يرمي بهاتفه على السرير حيث يبقى مستلقياً.

المشهد ٧
منزل ويليام

ويليام، يمارس تمارين سباحته الصباحية ذهاباً وإياباً في حوض السباحة في الخارج.
داخل بيته الكبير والفاخر، تأخذ صوفيا قياسات الصالون المزيّن بذوقٍ رفيع، وتدوّنها في دفترها. تساعدها في هذه المهمّة مدبرة المنزل.

بعد انتهائه من تمارينه، يخرج ويليام من حوض السباحة، يرتدي برنُساً ويدخل الصالون.

ويليام
بونجور

صوفيا
بونجور

ويليام
ويليام

صوفيا
صوفيا، من مكتب «بخعازي وبخعازي».

ويليام
sorry بس أنا مضطر إمشي. إذا فيني أعملّك brief سريع وبعدين بتكملي اللي عم تعملي.

صوفيا
أكيد.

ويليام
منشرب قهوة برّا.

على الشرفة، ويليام وصوفيا يحتسيان القهوة.
على طاولة الإفطار القريبة منهما وعاء مليء بالتفاح، بعض فطائر الكرواسون، سلطة فواكه، وعصير برتقال.

ويليام
...وأهم شي المكتبة تنعطى قيمتها، بدّي اياها عاهيدا الحيط،
وبدّي الـ wine cellar تكون على الحيط اللي بالوجّ، يعني الديكور
بدّو يدور بفَلَكُن.

صوفيا تدوّن الملاحظات على دفترها.

صوفيا
لاحظت إنه ما في TV، بدك حُط واحد؟

ويليام
أكيد لأ. ما معي هالقد مصاري.

صوفيا تبتسم.

ويليام
أنا حوّيص. أيمتى بتفرجيني شي؟

صوفيا
الأسبوع الجايي؟

ويليام
بكرا عشيّة.

يُلقي ويليام نظرة خاطفة على يديها، ويلاحظ أنها لا ترتدي محبس خطوبة أو زواج.

ويليام
بالـ Avalon عالثمانية ونص.
ما في لزوم لخرائط كاملة، كم سكيتش بيكفّوا.

ويليام يقف متأهباً.

ويليام
بالإذن، بس پليز إنتِ كمّلي ترويقتِك.

ويليام يأخذ من طاولة الإفطار تفاحة، يقضمها وهو يغادر، بينما صوفيا ما زالت تستوعب الأمر الواقع الذي فرض عليها.

المشهد ٨
عيادة جاك الخاصة

جاك يحاول الاتصال بصوفيا مجدداً. لا تجيب.
ينهض عن كرسيه ويتجه نحو صالة الاستقبال، حيث تعمل مساعدته على بعض الملفات.

جاك
فيي أعمُل مخابرة من تلفونِك؟

المساعدة

(تبدو مستغربة)

أوكي.

جاك
فيّ واحد بدّي مِتّو مصاري ما عم يردّ.كيف صايرة هالعالم ولو!

يأخذ هاتف المساعدة ويعود إلى مكتبه.

المشهد ٩
مكتب التصميم الداخلي

صوفيا تعمل على مشروع ويليام. يرن هاتفها.
لا تعرف رقم المتصل

صوفيا
ألو؟

جاك
صوفيا

صوفيا
مين معي؟

جاك
جاك

تقطع صوفيا الاتصال وتعود إلى العمل. جاك يتصل مجدداً، إلا أن صوفيا قد حوّلت هاتفها الى وضعية الصمت.

إقترب موعد اجتماعها مع مديرها، السيد بخعازي. تعاين ساعتها، ثم تنهض وتتوجّه الى مكتبه وتجلس أمامه.

صوفيا
موسيو بخعازي، بخصوص الليلة، مَنّي حاضرة!

المدير
قلت للشباب يساعدوكي بالمشروع! شو القصّة؟!

صوفيا
الـ projet حاضر. بس كرمال العشا وهيك، عم فكّر إنه...

المدير
صوفيا، ويليام زبون دقّيع، شوي pushy بس بيدفَع كاش.
وبتعرفي شو يعني زبون دقّيع هالإيام؟ يعني إله، أسطورة، من هودي يلّي انقرضوا مع الزمن.
فا بتزبطيلي جمالك عشية، ومتل الوردة بتكوني ثماني ونص إلا دقيقة بالـ Avalon عم تاكلي مع بسمة على وجّك. شي مرّة آكلة إنت وعم تضحكي؟!

المشهد ١٠
منزل جيهان، ليلاً

جيهان (٦٠ سنة)، والدة صوفيا، تشاهد التلفاز في غرفة الجلوس ذات الإضاءة الخافتة، بينما صوفيا في غرفتها تجهّز نفسها لموعد العشاء مع ويليام.

جاك يصل في سيارته إلى المبنى الذي تسكنه جيهان. راجين، ناطور المبنى، يرفع له حاجز المرور، سامحاً بدخوله.

تخرج صوفيا من غرفتها وتتأمل والدتها جيهان وهي جالسة هناك وحيدة. تشعر جيهان بوجود صوفيا، فتلتفت إليها وتتفاجأ بمظهرها المتأنّق.

صوفيا
باي ماما.

جيهان
مش بكّير شوي لنبلّش نضهر؟!

صوفيا
شغل ماما، مجبورة روح، باي.

في لوبي البناء جاك ينتظر المصعد. تفتح الأبواب وتخرج صوفيا. كلاهما يتفاجأ بوجود الآخر!

جاك
أها!

صوفيا
شو بدّك؟!

جاك
سلامتك.

صوفيا
إيه عال، كتّر خير الله.

تُكمـلُ صوفيـا طريقها من أمامه، فيمسـكها جاك من مرفقها.

جاك
صوفيا!

صوفيا
متّي فاضية جاك، عندي شغل!

جاك
صرنا نشتغل بالليل كمان، روعة!

صوفيا
ما عم إمزح، كتير مستعجلة.
إذا عندك شي تقوله، قوله عالسريع.

جاك
Sorry نسيت عيد زواجنا، حقّك علي.
بس إنو معقول تتركي البيت كرمال هيك شي؟!

صوفيا
ليـك! أوعك تجرّب تسـخّف الأمور متل عادتك! مشـاكلنا أعتق وأعمـق بكتيـر من هيك وإنت عارف. بـس هيدي كانت الـ cherry on top! (النقطـة للـي خلّت الكوب يطوف!)

جاك
إنه صوفيا وينك عايشة؟ منّا الوحيدين!
فتّحي عيونِك، إتطلّعي حواليكِ. في شي couple ما عندو مشاكل؟!
إسألي صاحباتِك.

صوفيا
ما بقا بدي إسمعا هيدي الأسطوانة! فهام! مني مثل غير نسوان،
ولا عندي ولاد لضحّي أو سد بوزي كرمالن!
وبصراحة؟ كنت كتير مبسوطة بحياتي قبلك.

جاك
خبّرتي إمّك؟!

صوفيا
أكيد، مش أحسن ما تفكر إنّا عايشين شهر عسل؟
وإنتِ هالسنة نايم عالصوفا أكثر ما نايم حدّي!

جاك
إي، الصوفا ما بتنئ.

ضغط صوفيا يرتفع بسرعة. ترفع حقيبتها لضربه بها، لكنها تتردّد في آخر لحظة.

جاك

Sorry, sorry وحياة الله ما قصدي.

صوفيا تحاول تهدئة نفسها.

صوفيا

ليك جاك، خلّينا ناخد مسافة، وكل واحد يفكّر مظبوط شو بدّو. عالأرجح إنه مَنّا لبعض.

جاك

أنا ما تجوّزت لطلّق!

صوفيا

روعة! بس بتأمّل يكون عندك سبب أذكى من هيدا لنضلّ سوا.

تربتُ على كتفه وتمشي في حال سبيلها.

جاك

صوفيا، صوفيا!

تسير صوفيا نحو سيارتها المركونة في الموقف. جاك يتبعها، فتستقلّ السيارة بسرعة. يقف في طريقها ليمنعها من المغادرة. تنطلق مسرعةً وكأنها مستعدة لدهسه فيقفز بعيداً عن طريقها. يركض جاك إلى سيارته. تتوقف صوفيا عند بوابة موقف الكاراج.

صوفيا

Rajin, keep him waiting. I don't want him following me.
(راجين، خلّيه ينطر. ما بدي ياه يلحقني)

راجين

Sure ma'am. **(حاضر مدام)**

تَخرجُ صوفيا من موقف السيارات ويُغلَقُ الحاجز خلفها. يصل جاك بسيارته على عجلة.

جاك

What's going on? **(شو عم بصير؟)**

راجين

Sorry Sir, it's not opening. **(بعتذر إستاذ، ما عم تفتح)**

جاك

Rajin, open it. **(راجين، فتاح)**

راجين

It's not working. **(ما عم تفتح)**

جاك
(راجين، والله بكسرا، فتاح) Rajin, I will break it, I swear.

راجين يتظاهر بمحاولة فتح الحاجز، لكنه لا يفلح في ذلك.يتراجع جاك بسيارته قليلا ويرمق راجين نظرة كما لو كان مصمماً على كسر الحاجز. راجين يفتح الحاجز في اللحظة الأخيرة، فينطلق جاك مسرعاً.
يلحقُ جاك بسيارة صوفيا بسرعة، مناوراً بين السيارات، ويبدأ بالتزمير دون توقف، متعقّباً إياها لبعض الوقت.

ترى صوفيا سيارة شرطة مركونة على جانب الطريق أمامها، وبداخلها شرطيان. توقِفُ سيارتها بجانبهما، فيتوقّف جاك خلفها ظنّاً منه أنها توقّفت للتحدث معه، فيترجّل من سيارته.

صوفيا
بونسوار

الشرطي
أهلا

صوفيا
الشبّ اللي بالسيارة ورايي لاحقني وعم يزنّخ علي،
بليز وقفوا عند حدّه.

الشرطي
ما تعتلي هم، هلّق منهتمّلك فيه.

يترجّل الشرطيان من السيارة ويتّجهان نحو جاك. تنطلق صوفيا بسيّارتها وتلوّح لجاك بيدها، بينما ترى في مرآتها الخلفية الشرطيان وهما يتحققان من أوراق جاك.

جاك
يا عمي مني عم زنّخ عالمرا....والله هيدي مرتي!

المشهد ١١
مطعم Avalon

تصل صوفيا إلى الطاولة حيث يجلس ويليام بانتظارها.

صوفيا
بونسوار

ويليام ينهض، يسحب لها الكرسي لتجلس عليه، ثم يعود إلى مكانه.

ويليام
تأخرتي.

صوفيا تنظر إلى ساعتها.

صوفيا
الساعة ٨:٣٠!

ويليام
معي ٨:٣٤! سمحيلي بساعتك.

صوفيا
Pardon?! (عفواً؟!)

ويليام
ساعتك.

تناوله ساعتها. ويليام يأخذها ويضبطها لتتطابق تماماً مع وقته.

ويليام
إذا رح نشتغل سوا لازم يكون وقتك على وقتي.

يعيد لها الساعة بينما هي في حالة ذهول!
يظهر النادل وفي يده زجاجة نبيذ يقدّمها لويليام.

النادل
Chablis Grand Cru.

يسكب القليل في كأس ويليام ليتذوّقه.

النادل
بتحبّوا مشّي الأكل؟

صوفيا
الـ menu بليز

ويليام
طلبتلّك.

ويليام يومئ للنادل لكي يسكب بعضاً من النبيذ في كأس صوفيا، التي لا تزال تحاول استيعاب الموقف. وكأنها تقول لنفسها: «شو هال control freak هيدا»!

Cut to

One hour later

بعض الأطباق الفارغة أمامهما. ويليام يراجع تفاصيل المشروع المرسومة بينما صوفيا تشرحها له.

صوفيا
... ومنفوّت بالمكتبة des touches de nacres[1]

ويليام
بحبّ الـ Mother of pearl
بس ما بيعطي شوي على Art Deco؟

صوفيا
حسب كيف منستعمله. الـ mother of pearl الغامق بي قلب الستانلس من لونه، رح يعطيه
a glimpse of shine in a very still surrounding.
(لمعة صغيرة بالحديد القاسي للي حواليه)

ويليام
هم!
ما بيعطي إنطباع إنّو شوي ناعم؟

صوفيا
بالعكس، كأنّك عم بتقول عن حدا، كتير رجّال بس حسّاس بنفس الوقت. إلّا إذا ما بيلبقلك هالشي!

ويليام يبتسم تقديراً لمحاولتها الناجحة بإقناعه عن طريق العبث بمشاعره. يعود النادل مع طبقين من ريزوتو الكمأة (truffle risotto).

صوفيا
هالكتب اللي بالمكتبة، ديكور ولّا...؟

ويليام
ولّا.

صوفيا
واو!

ويليام
إنتِ ما بتقري؟

صوفيا
إنّو تغيّرت الإيام، صار كلّه عالتليفون. وإذا الواحد بدّو جواب عا شي، بغوغلو.

ويليام
أجوبة؟!

ويليام يضحك.

١ ورق اللولو

الكتاب الذكي بخلّيكي تسألي حالك أسئلة، وأكيد الجواب عليهن
مش هون (التليفون).
فرّقي حالك عن الباقيين.
الزهرة الحلوة بتعبّي العين، بس اللي ريحتا طيبة،
بتفوت لهون.(يشير إلى صدره).

تتذوّق القليل من طبق الريزوتو، من الواضح أن مذاقه يعجبها.

صوفيا
مممممم!! شو بتشتغل حضرتك؟

ويليام
حضرتي! هه. بستثمر بأشيا مش عاديّة.

صوفيا
متل شو؟

ويليام
يلّي عم تاكليه مثلاً.

صوفيا
ريزوتو؟!

ويليام
يلّي على وجّ الريزوتو.

صوفيا
Truffle?

ويليام
White truffle.

صوفيا
هيدا شغلك؟!

ويليام يومئ برأسه موافقاً.

صوفيا
هلّق إنتِ عايش هيك من هيدا الشي؟!

ويليام
كيف «هيك» يعني؟

صوفيا
واضح إنك بتنكسر بآخر الشهر على كم مية دولار.

يضحكان

ويليام
عندي كذا شركة. بس بتعرفي قديش حقا الكمشة من هول؟

صوفيا
٥٠ دولار؟

ويليام
زيديلُن صفرين.

صوفيا
٥٠٠٠ دولار؟!!!

ويليام
وما بتلاقي. وبالسوق السودا بعد أغلى.

تغصُّ صوفيا بالريزوتو عندما تسمع الرقم.

ويليام
واضح إنِّك بتحبّي شغلك.

صوفيا
قبل ما إكتشف إنّو كمشة الـ truffle بـ ٥٠٠٠ دولار

ويليام يضحك على تعليقها، ويرفع كأسه.

ويليام
كاسك دوموازيل داغر

صوفيا
مدام

ويليام
آآآ مجوّزة؟!

صوفيا

تهز رأسها بتردد

يمكن... ما بعرف.

ويليام
ما بتعرفي! حلوا!... ليه ما بتغوغليا؟!

Cut to

إنتهى لقاء العشاء، ويليام وصوفيا يسيران باتجاه باب مطعم Avalon.

ويليام
خلصوا الخرايط؟

صوفيا
مبارح.

يضحكان.

صوفيا
بشتغلن بكرا، يعني بعد بكرا بيخلصوا.

ويليام
الساعة ١٠ عندي بالبيت

تحضر سيارة صوفيا.

ويليام
تصبحي على خير

تصعد في سيارتها وتغادر.

المشهد ١٢
عيادة جاك الخاصة

جاك يُعالج أحد المرضى، ويشدُّ ساقه.
سارحاً في أفكاره، يشدُّ ساق المريض أكثر من اللازم.

المريض
آخ آخ

جاك
عفواً

ربيع يقف على باب العيادة.

ربيع
حكيني كلمة.

جاك يمشي صوبه إلى الباب.

بصفتي حكيم مرتك بذكرك إنا مفروض تكون ovulating حالياً.
يعني الليلة ليلتك، إذا حابب تعملّنا ولد.

جاك
روعة! ما في دقيقة معيّنة كمان؟!
ليك ركّبلي هاوِس بفرد مرّة: مهيَّج، مش مهيّج.

ربيع
إذا مقصّر وبدّك زنّيفة، نحنا حاضرين.

جاك
لحاس طيزي.

ربيع
شو عامِل الليلة؟ تعا حضار فوتبول.

جاك
ما بعرف، بحكيك.

ربيع

ينسحب ممازحاً.

مين رح يعمل واحد الليلة؟

جاك يتظاهر بأنّه سوف يركله، فيبتعد ربيع مسرعاً.

المشهد ١٣
استديو يوغا، ليلاً

صوفيا جالسة بين الجمع في مكانها المعتاد في حصة اليوغا.
يدخل جاك مرتدياً ملابس رياضية، وعلى كتفه منشفة.
يجلس على الأرض بجانب صوفيا.

صوفيا
شو عم تعمل هون؟!

جاك
يوغا!

صوفيا
جاك!

جاك
ما عم بتردّي عا تليفوناتي، وما بدّي روح عبيت إمّك.

تعلن المعلمة افتتاح الصف.
جاك يحاول أن يؤدي حركة معينة، غير أن مظهره يبدو مضحكاً.

جاك
قال ربيع إنّو حالياً وقت تِحبلي وإنّو لازم نعملا.

صوفيا
عال عملوها سوا.

جاك
بلا سآلتِك!

تفتح مُعلّمة اليوغا عيناً واحدةً وترمقُ جاك بنظرةٍ صارمة.
جاك يرفع ذراعيه فوق رأسه في وضعية الشجرة متظاهراً بالتأمل.
عندما تُغمض المُعلّمة عينها، يهمس مجدداً لصوفيا.

جاك
شو؟ صوفيا؟

صوفيا
عن جد جايي تِحكيني بالموضوع هلّق، هون؟!

جاك
أنا قلت هون بتكون أعصابك مرتاحة.

صوفيا لا تجيب، وتحاول السيطرة على أعصابها.
جاك يأخذ نفساً على طريقة اليوغا.

صوفيا
فِلّ! هلّق!

جاك
وعديني تخلصي وتِلحقيني.

صوفيا
إنت عأي كوكب عايش؟ عن جد؟! ملاحظ إنّي تركت البيت؟!
ما فهمت؟ كيف جايي تحكيني بولد؟!

جاك
مش إنت بدّك ولد؟!

جاك يحاول تأدية حركة صعبة يقوم بها جميع من في الصّف.

صوفيا
مبلا، بس حتّى الحيوانات بيعملوا رقصة صغيرة قبل ما «ينـت....» !
حلّ مشاكلك قبل ما تعرض خدماتك العضوية!

تفتح معلّمة اليوغا عينيها من جديد.

معلّمة اليوغا
Sir, you have to leave!
(موسيو بدي أطلب منك تترك الصف!)

جاك
Why? I'm in the moment.
(ليه؟ أنا كتير عايشا.)

جاك على الأرض في وضعيّة تمدد قاسية. صوفيا تقف.

صوفيا
No, no, let him stay...
(لا لا، خلّيه)

صوفيا تكبس كبسة قويّة على ظهر جاك، فيُمزق كعب فخذِه.

جاك
آخ آخ آخ

صوفيا
(... بما إنه عايشا!) Since he's in the moment

صوفيا تغادر بينما جاك ممدد على الأرض، يتأوّه من الألم.

المشهد ١٤
منزل ويليام

يدق جرس الباب، مدبرة المنزل تفتح الباب، إنها صوفيا.

صوفيا
(بونجور) Good morning

مدبرة المنزل
(بونجور مدام) Good morning ma'am

صوفيا تدخل.

صوفيا
(موسيو ويليام موجود؟) Is Mr. William here?

تلقي صوفيا نظرة خاطفة على نفسها في المرآة، وترتّب شعرها. تلفت نظرها باقة زهور رائعة موضوعة على البوفيه. تلمس إحدى أوراقها، ثم تلتقط بهاتفها صورة للباقة.

يصل ويليام مرتدياً بذلة، وجاهزاً لمغادرة المنزل.

ويليام
صباح الخير

صوفيا
بونجور شو سبسيال هالوردات!

ويليام
جدّ علي اجتماع، لازم كون بالـ downtown بعد نص ساعة.
فينا نأجّل، إلّا إذا بترافقيني ومنحكي عالطريق.

صوفيا
ما رح توصل عالوقت، كتير عجقة.

ويليام
يا قليلة الإيمان...

المشهد ١٥
يخت ويليام في البحر

ويليام وصوفيا في يخته الفاخر الكبير متّجهَين بسرعة نحو بيروت.

صوفيا
هاي أوّل مرّة بعمل presentation بالبحر!

ويليام
Time is money.

ويليام ينظر إلى التصميمات، بينما صوفيا تشرحها له. يرن هاتف ويليام.

ويليام
Sorry

يرد على الهاتف.

إيه، طوني؟

المشهد ١٦
قاعة اجتماعات في مكتب فاخر

طوني في قاعة الاجتماعات حيث يجتمع أعضاء مجلس الإدارة، وقد تنحّى جانباً ليتكلّم بصوت منخفض.

طوني
وين صرت؟

ويليام
واصل. شو بيك بتضلّك متوتّر؟

طوني
في شي غلط.

ويليام
إرتاح، هاي الشركة بتنباع لمين أنا بقرّر، وبالسعر يلّلي أنا بقررو.
إتركن يحلموا، ما في نصاب.

طوني
سليم هون.

ويليام
سليم عاطينا تفويض!

طوني
مش إذا حضر شخصيّاً!

ويليام يصمت.

طوني
منّي مطمّن ويليام، فيا لعبة.

يصل اليخت إلى مرفأ «زيتونة باي» في وسط بيروت.

ويليام
واصل.

ويليام ينهي المكالمة.

صوفيا
مشاكل بالشغل؟

ويليام
شوية suspense بس بالآخر البطل عطول بيربح.

صوفيا تضحك.
ويليام يتهيّأ للنزول من اليخت، قبل ان يتوقف ويستدير صوبها.

ويليام
شو عاملة الليلة؟ تعي سهري.

صوفيا
مرسي، ما في.

ويليام
عامل جَمعة وفي ناس مهم تتعرّفي علين.

صوفيا
عندي شي.

ويليام
إلغي!

صوفيا
ما بتصوّر.

ويليام
عبالك تضلّك موظّفة كل حياتك؟!
اللي رح يكونوا الليلة فيهن يغيّرولك حياتك.

At 8:30 p.m. sharp, and bring your ambitions with you.
(كوني ٨:٣٠ عالتمام، وما تنسي تجيبي طموحك معك)

المشهد ١٧
قاعة اجتماعات في مكتب فاخر

ويليام يترأّس اجتماع مجلس الإدارة المؤلّف من ١٠ أشخاص.
جمال، أحد أعضاء مجلس الإدارة، يتولى قيادة المعارضة ضد ويليام.

جمال
الجماعة حاطّين ١٠٠ مليون دولار عالطاولة، وأكترية الأعضاء موافقين عهالبيعة.

يبرُز مستنداً.

هيدي التواقيع

ويليام
١٠٠ مليون! بتحب الرخص. الشركة بتسوا أكتر بكتير!

جمال
مش هالإيام، ومع مشكلة الـسيولة بالسوق.
بتعرف شو مشكلتك ويليام؟ إنّك عايش عالأمجاد.

ويليام
عالقليلة عندي أمجاد! أمجاد كلكن إغتنيتوا من وراها.

سليم
ويليام ما حدا عم يقلّل من قيمة تعبك، بس الإيام بطّلت متل قبل.

ويليام
سليم، إنت أكتر واحد عارف إنّو بس يركب الـ deal
مع الصينيين، السهم رح يرجع يفرقع.

سليم
صرلنا ٦ أشهر عم منركّب هالـ deal وما كان يركب.

ويليام
إنت قلتا، الإيام بطّلت متل الأوّل.
الـ deal صار بدّو تعب أكتر، بس جايي، قصّة وقت.

سليم
ما عندي وقت.
خسران كتير مصاري بالبورصة وعاوزني كاش هلّق.

المشهد ١٨
منزل ويليام

في السهرة، يجتمع حوالي ١٢ شخصاً حول حوض السباحة.
ويليام يتكلّم مع طوني.

ويليام
جمال عم يعمل كل هالشي ليقعد محلّي، بدّو الكرسي.
بس سليم شو بدّو؟!

طوني
كاش؟

ويليام
كذّاب. هوّي بالزمانات خبّرني بلسانو إنّو الشغلة الوحيدة اللي ما بيعملا بحياتو هي البورصة. في شي تاني، أكيد جمال واعده بشي.

في هذه اللحظة تطلّ صوفيا من الباب بكامل أناقتها. ويليام يتوجّه نحوها مبتسماً وممازحاً.

ويليام
تأخّرتي.

صوفيا تُريه معصمها وأنها ترتدي ساعة مختلفة عن التي ضبطها على وقته.

صوفيا
غيّرت الساعة.

ويليام
طالعة بتعقّدي.

صوفيا
مرسي.

ويليام
تعي لعرّفِك.

توجه بها صوب شخصين يتحدثان.

ويليام
الدكتور سلمان، أشهر من أن يُعرّف.
والدكتور عمر مؤسس ومدير «مركز سرطان الأطفال».
أو صار لازم عيّطلك معالي الوزير؟

د. عمر
إنت شو عرّفك؟

ويليام

ولو مايسترو؟! على كل حال كثير بتلبقلك.
صوفيا مصمّمة ديكور من الطراز الأوّل. عندا ذوق كتير رفيع، عم تشتغلّي حالياً عالبيت.

صوفيا

مسا الخير.

د. عمر

عظيم، إذا هيك بتصمّميلنا الغرف الجديدة للأولاد بالمستشفى.

ويليام

أوف، بهالسرعة معاليك؟!

د. عمر

ويليام، إذا إنت بتقول عنا منيحة يعني ممتازة. بعرف ذوقك.

ويليام

تسلم دكتور.

صوفيا

موسيو ويليام بيحب يكبّرا شوي.

يضحكون. يحضرُ النادل صينيّة من كؤوس الشمبانيا. ويليام يأخذ كأسَي شمبانيا ويقدّم واحداً لصوفيا.

* أغنية*«Temptation» لميشال غوروفيتش تسمع في الخلفية.

ويليام

يخاطبُ صوفيا همساً.

بدنا نشدّ حالنا. شويّة ثقة بالنّفس.

صوفيا

ثقة بالنّفس في، بس الـ ego تبعك ما عندي ياه.

ويليام

غلطانة كتير، هودي وجّين لفرد عملة.
عندك ego أكتر منّي. للحقيقة، عندك كتير مواهب نايمة،
وأنا رح وعّيلك ياها. تشيرز!

صوفيا تنظر إليه للحظة وتهزّ رأسها. ثمّ تمُدّ كأسها له.

صوفيا

تشيرز!

ويليام

وفيكي توقفي تعيطيلي موسيو.

تستمر السهرة حتى وقت متأخر من الليل.

من بعيد، ويليام يراقب صوفيا وهي تتحدث مع أحد الضيوف، ويراقب لباقتها، حركات يديها اللطيفة، شفتيها المرسومتين وهي تبتسم بأدب لمخاطبها. تجول صوفيا بنظرها في أرجاء المكان، تلتقي عيناها بعيني ويليام الذي يراقبها.

يتبادلان النظرات للحظات طويلة وكأنهما الشخصان الوحيدان في السهرة.

Cut to black

*امسح لسماع الاغنية

المشهد ١٩
منزل ويليام

ويليام يمارس سباحته الصباحية اليومية.
يصل صديقه الدوكتور فؤاد (٥٠ عاماً) وينتظره حتى ينتهي.
ويليام يخرج من حوض السباحة ويتوجّه إلى ركن الإفطار حيث يوجد وعاء كامل من التفاح ووجبة إفطار طازجة. يتناول فنجانين من القهوة، يقدّم أحدهما لفؤاد، ويجلس مواجهاً له.

ويليام
ما في شغل اليوم؟

فؤاد
مبلا. بس قلت بشوفك شوي. كيفك؟

ويليام
كتير منيح. ماشي عالصين بكرا، بتجي؟ بشرفك.

فؤاد يهزّ رأسه نفياً.

ويليام
عن جدّ مشّي. بطعميك شوربة إجرين دجاج، أكلة.

د. فؤاد
ما فيي روح... ولا إنتَ!

ويليام
ليه بقا؟!

د. فؤاد
لأنّو طلعت نتيجة الزرع. والدرنة اللي كنّا مفكرينا كيس، ما طلعت كيس.

ويليام
شو طلعت؟!

فؤاد لا يجيب.

ويليام
فؤاد؟! بشرفك إحكي، قد ما تكون بشعة مش قد هالشي اللي معيّشني اياه.... نطوق!

د. فؤاد
كانسر

ويليام
الوضع سيّئ؟

د. فؤاد
سيّئ

ويليام
قدّيه؟

فؤاد لا يجيب.

لك إحكي!!!

د. فؤاد
الأسوأ، رابع مرحلة.

نظرة ويليام وكأن الزمن يقف به.
في عقله، تتوالى بسرعة سلسلة من المشاهد الارتجاعية:
مستلقياً داخل جهاز التصوير بالرنين المغناطيسي.
يسبح تحت الماء في حوض سباحة.
طفل يولد لتوّه.
أمّهُ تناديه باسمه وهو طفل يقوم بأولى خطواته.
يضرب كيس مُلاكمة بكامل قواه.
يمارس الحب مع امرأة جميلة.
بعمر ١٢ سنة، يجلس في عربة خشبية يدوية الصنع ذات عجلات صغيرة، تنحدر بسرعة باتجاه جدار. يصرخ ويغمض عينيه قبل الاصطدام.

Fade to black

four months later

ويليام شاحب، متعب وضعيف، جالس في كرسيه مقابل دوكتور فؤاد في نفس المكان والوضعية اللذين كانا فيها عند سماعه خبر مرضه.

د. فؤاد
عم تنزل عالماي؟

ويليام
تسئ.

د. فؤاد
بس Willy، شوية تمارين عالناعم بتفيدك. ماتيو بساعدك.

ويليام
إنزل طبّس بالماي من بعد ما قضيت حياتي آكل البيسين؟!

د. فؤاد
لازم تقوّي حالك.

يخرج ماتيو (٣٠ سنة) وهو ممرّض ويليام، مثلي، ذو بنية قوية، حاملاً فنجان قهوة لفؤاد.

ويليام
تقوّيني لشو؟! لتطولّي عذابي يعني؟! فظيعين انتو الدكاترة!
بيبقى المريض عم ينشوي عالنار، وبدال ما تخلّصوا بسرعة،
بتصيروا تقلّبوه.

(يقوم بحركة الشوّى الذي يقلّب اللحمة عالنار)

Rare, medium, well done!

فؤاد وماتيو يضحكان.

ويليام
بدّك تعمل شي منيح، زيد هالمورفينات شوي. عالقليلة هودي
بيسكّتولي الأصوات اللّي هون (رأسه)

ماتيو
إي، إي، قد ما عاليين هالأصوات أنا كمان عم إسمعن.
زدلنا مورفين دكتور، وإذا فيك شويّة mari كمان.

يضحكون.

ويليام
لازم لهّي حالي بشي!!!

د. فؤاد
القعدة مش عم تساعدك، لازملك علاج فيزيائي، بتتغيّر أفكارك.
رح إبعتلك واحد عالبيت.

ويليام
وحدة.

ماتيو
سمعته كتير منيح، الدكتور قال «واحد».

ويليام
وحدة، شقرا، طويلة، بزازا كبار.

ماتيو
إسما يوسف.

ويليام يصفن مطوّلاً، ثم يبدو وكأن فكرةً خطرت له.

ويليام
أنا بعرف مين رح تبعت!!

المشهد ٢٠
منزل ويليام

جاك يصل في سيارته ويركنها في الممرّ الخاص بمنزل ويليام.

Cut to

على الشرفة، ويليام مستلقياً على أريكة يقرأ كتاباً، وبجانبه زجاجة كونياك «XO». يرتشف كأساً ويدخن سيغاريللو يصل ماتيو.

ماتيو
Non, non. (لأ، لأ)

ويليام يتناول صورة فوتوغرافية موضوعة على الطاولة إلى جانبه، ويضعها في الكتاب إلى حيث وصل في القراءة. يضع الكتاب جانباً.

ويليام
Si, si. (مبلا، مبلا)

ماتيو
Mais tu es complètement fou! (إنت مجنون رسمياً!)

ويليام
من شو خايف مثلاً؟ أعمل كانسر؟

ماتيو
ويليام!!

ويليام
تعا قعود هون شراب كاسي، يلّا.

ماتيو يقترب ويجلس قربه.

ماتيو
Non, non, j'aime pas. (لا لا ما بحب.)

ويليام
يلّا!

ويليام يقرّب الكأس من فم ماتيو. ماتيو يأخذ الكأس، يشمّ الكونياك قبل أن يأخذ منه جرعة صغيرة. يمتعض من الطعم.

ماتيو!
مممممم!

يمد له السيغاريللو.

ويليام
يلّا

ماتيو، الذي لا يزال ممتعضاً من مذاق الكونياك، يهز أصبعه رافضاً السيغاريللو.

ويليام
يلّا!!!

ماتيو يُذعن ويأخذ مجّة من السيغاريللو، فيبدأ بالسعال وتدمع عيناه. ويليام يضحك.

Cut to

في الممر، يترجّل جاك من سيارته ويأخذ وقته في التمعّن بمنظر المنزل والحديقة. يمشي ببطء نحو الباب ويقرع الجرس.

Cut back

مدبرة المنزل تصل إلى حيث يستلقي ويليام وتخاطبه.

مدبرة المنزل
Sir, there's a guy at the door "for massage."
(إستاذ ويليام، في شاب عالباب كرمال المسّاج)

ويليام

مشيراً إليها بيده أن ترميه.

In the trash!
(عالزبالة!)

تضع مدبرة المنزل يدها على فمها وتضحك ضحكة مكتومة على إجابة ويليام.

ماتيو يتبع مدبرة المنزل ليرحّب بـ جاك.

جاك يقف في غرفة الجلوس يتأمل كل شيء. تتفحّص عيناه اللوحات والديكور: علبة سيجار، تلسكوب، تمثال لامرأة عارية، إبريق كونياك، وخزانة كتب ضخمة.يمرّر جاك أصبعه بخفّة على صدر المرأة العارية.

ماتيو
مرحبا

جاك يتفاجأ ويسحب بسرعة يده عن صدر التمثال، ماتيو يضحك.

جاك
مرحبا.

ماتيو
تفضّل معي إذا بتريد.

جاك يتبع ماتيو إلى الشرفة ويتفاجأ برؤية ويليام يشرب ويدخن.

جاك
مرحبا

ويليام
أهلا

جاك
مسيو ويليام؟

ويليام

بنبرةٍ جادة

مين حضرتك؟!

جاك
باعتني لعندك دوكتور فؤاد.

ويليام
بخصوص السيفون اللي عم يروّح؟
ماتيو، دِلّ المعلم عالتواليت.

جاك متفاجئاً

جاك
لا أنا مش سمكري، أنا معالج فيزيائي، بس قلّي في شخص مريض، مش حضرتك؟

ويليام
شو شايف بني؟! عم دخّن وأشرب كونياك.

جاك
لأ.... بسّ.... آهه..

ويليام
شو باك عم تأتئ! شدّ حالك!!

ماتيو يضحك ويحضر لنجدة جاك.

ماتيو
William arrête! (ويليام، وقّف!)

جاك، مستغرباً، يتردّد قليلاً قبل أن يجلس.

ماتيو
شو بتحب تاخذ؟

جاك
مرسي ما تتعذب.

ويليام
كيف ما تتعذب، ضيّفو شي... جبلو لبن.

جاك يتفاجأ مجدداً عندما يسمع أن ويليام يريد أن يقدم له اللبن.
ينظر إلى ماتيو مستنجداً، لا يعرف ما إذا كان ويليام جاداً في ما يقول.

جاك
والله ما فيّي.

ويليام
مبلا، مبلا، طازة، روعة للمصارين.

جاك
لا عن جد مرسي.

ويليام
جبلو كاسة لبن.

ماتيو
Méchant William!
(شرير ويليام!)

Cut to

المشهد ٢١

مكتب التصميم الداخلي

صوفيا جالسة على مكتبها تعمل، تسمع طرقاً على الباب.
يدخل عامل التوصيل ليسلّمها باقة زهور.

العامل

مدام صوفيا؟

صوفيا

نعم

العامل

بتمضيلي هون عملي معروف؟

صوفيا توقّع. العامل يضع الباقة على المكتب.

صوفيا

ما فيه بطاقة؟

العامل

والله أنا ما بعرف شي يا ست، قالولي وصّلن.

المشهد ٢٢

منزل ويليام، غرفة النوم

ويليام مستلقياً على سرير تدليك قابل للطيّ أحضره جاك.
جاك يحرّك ذراعي ويليام وساقيه.

ويليام

بتعملّك بالنهار شي سبع تمان ساعات؟

جاك

مينيموم

ويليام

نيّالا صاحبتك، بيطلعلا كل يوم مسّاج.

جاك

مرتي

ويليام

وإنت عندك حجّة تفركلا رقبتا.

جاك يبتسم للفكرة.

ويليام
بدّن فرك رقبة، ما هيك؟

جاك لا يجيب.

ويليام
مع هيك إيدين أكيد عاملتلك تمثال.

جاك
إي، قـد مـا كبير التمثال، ما عاد ساعنا البيـت، فا قامت فلّت.

ويليام
ولازم هنّيك أو عزّيك؟

جاك
عفواً؟!

ويليام
sorry بس إنو إذا الواحد مرته ما بتنطاق، بكون انكتبله عمر جديد.

ملامح وجه جاك تؤكّد أنه حزين لمغادرتها.

ويليام
بس... إذا بعدَك بتحِبّا، مشكلة.

جاك بسرعة يجيب دون تفكير.

جاك
بحبّا.

ويليام
أكيد؟!

جاك
إي أكيد!

ويليام
مش معقولة تكون إنه تعوّدت عليها؟!
كثير أوقات الناس بتلخبط بين الحب والعادة.

جاك
لأ مني ملخبط، بحبّا!

ويليام
طيب وإذا سألتك شو أكثر شي بتحبّه فيا؟ شو أول شي بيجي عا راسك؟

تمر ثوان وجاك لا يجد الجواب.

ويليام
ممممم...! طيب وهي؟
بعتذر أنا عم إسأل، فيك ما تجاوب.

جاك
لا، مش مشكل. هي شو؟

ويليام
ليه فلّت؟ عندا حدا ثاني؟

جاك
أكيد لأ!

ملامح ويليام وهو يراقب جاك، مستوعباً طريقة تفكيره، تجعل جاك غير مرتاح.

جاك
شو؟!

ويليام
أبداً.

جاك
لأ، قول.

ويليام
ما شي، بس حبيت overdose الثقة للي عندك ياها.

جاك
منا ثقة زايدة، مرتي وبعرفا عن الغايب.

ويليام
مممم! نحنا بوجود رجّال بيعرف المرا عن الغايب!

جاك
طبعاً.

ويليام
والله! وليه تركت البيت فإذن؟...
Don't take her for granted my friend
(ما تنام عا حرير يا صديقي)
السوفتوير عندا مختلف كلّياً عنّك، الكومبيوتر تبعك يمكن يقراه،
بس مش أكيد يستوعبه!

Cut to

المشهد ٣٣
مكتب التصميم الداخلي

صوفيا تتأمل الباقة التي وصلتها وكأنها تستشبه بشيءٍ ما.
تلتقط هاتفها، تدخل الى غاليري الصور فيه وتتصفحها، ثم تتوقف عند صورة الباقة التي التقطتها في منزل ويليام. هو نفس نوع الأزهار.

تفكّر للحظات قبل أن تقرر الاتصال بويليام، ولكن الاتصال يفشل، كما لو كان ويليام قد حظر رقمها.

Cut back

المشهد ٣٤
منزل ويليام

ماتيو مرافقاً جاك إلى الباب، يُسمَع صوت سُعال ويليام من الغرفة المجاورة.

جاك
جرّبت قد ما فيي ضهّرلو البلغم من الروايا. بس مش معقول تخلّيه يدخّن، عم ينتحر.

ماتيو
ما بيقنع.

جاك
وعم يعمل علاج كيميائي؟

ماتيو
رافض.

جاك
عكل حال تركه يرتاح هلّق، دايماً أول جلسة بتكون شوي قاسية.

المشهد ٣٥
المرفأ، قارب صيد، ليلاً

ندي وربيع ينتظران جاك في المركب. جاك يصل راكضاً حاملاً أغراضه.

ندي
يا أخي وينك؟

جاك

Sorry, sorry, sorry

بس عندي هونيك مريض جديد، منيوك ومفلسف،
بِقي ساعة يقرط حكي ونظريات.

جاك كالعادة يضع هاتفه إلى جانب الهواتف الأخرى في الصندوق المجاور لمقعد القبطان.

جاك

رح روح غيّر تيابي.

ندي يحاول تشغيل القارب أكثر من مرّة لكنه يفشل.

Cut to

An hour later

القارب لم ينطلق جرّاء عطلٍ ما، فيبقى راسياً في المرفأ، الشباب يشربون البيرة، جاك يبدو ساهياً.

ربيع

ألو؟! وينك؟!

جاك

عم فكّر بهيدا الزلمي. في مصاري ما بتاكلا النيران، فيلا مع pool
بتجنّن، وبليلة ما فيا ضو قمر، كانسر. بوف، انتهت حياته!

ندي

ياي شو دراما كوين!

جاك

إذا قالولك عندَك ٦ أشهر تعيش، شو بتعمل؟

ندي

أوّل شي بعمل بلوك لمرتي لما تزعجني. وبعبّي الboat كحول
ونسوان وبموت سكران بين فخاذن!

جاك

ما أسخفَك!

ندي

يا أخي ليه بدّك تفقسلنا سهرتنا؟! شو أنا جبتلّه الكانسر
للزلمة؟! ما معا حق صوفيا تتركك؟!

جاك

كول خرا.

ربيع
شو جديدكن دخلك؟

جاك
جديدنا؟! ألبوم duo، واتفاقية الطلاق.

ربيع
عفكرة وقبل ما إنسى، التقيت بمديرك نبيل وقلّي مهاجر على كندا.
وإنه عم يحكوا فيك جدّياً لتكون رئيس قسم العلاج الفيزيائي محلّه.

جاك

(محتفلاً)

وووهوووو! Yesss
أصلاً بعتلي واتساب اليوم بس نسيت إفتحه.

ندي يقف قرب المقود حيث يضع الجميع هواتفهم.

جاك
بشرفك ناولني هالتلفون لشوفه.

جاك في وسط نشوته وانشغاله بالخبر السعيد، لا ينتبه إلى ندي يغمز ربيع، قبل أن يلتقط هاتف ويرميه بسرعة نحو جاك بحركة مقصودة.

ندي
كموش

جاك يفشل في التقاط هاتفه الذي يصطدم بحافة القارب ثم يقع في الماء. جاك يشتعل غضباً ويركض في أرجاء القارب صارخاً في وجه ندي. ندي وربيع يتصرّفان ببرودة أعصاب زائدة.

ربيع
يا زلمة كيف بتعمل هيك؟!

ندي
أنا؟! الحق عليه، هوي اللي مش منتبه.

جاك
الحق علي أنا؟ يا حيوان صرت قايلّك ألف مرّة ما تكبّ التلفون!

ندي
بشرفك جاك، خود حقّه وما تسمّعني صوتك!

جاك، وبشكل هستيري، يرمي بشبكة صيد في الماء محاولاً أن يصطاد الهاتف.

ندي وربيع يعجزان عن ضبط نفسيهما أمام هذا الموقف وينفجران من الضحك. جاك يدرك أن الأمر كان مجرد مزحة، فيهجم عليهما ويوجه لهما اللكمات.

جاك
شو كبّيت بالماي؟!

ندي
تلفون لعبة

ندي يناول جاك هاتفه. جاك يضرب ندي بلكمةٍ على كتفه.

جاك
حيوان!

المشهد ٣٦
مقهى جاك وصوفيا المفضّل

يبدأ حديث جاك وصوفيا فيما تجول الكاميرا في أرجاء المقهى حيث أشخاص جالسون إلى طاولات، منهم من يقرأ، البعض الآخر يتحدّث، ومنهم من يعمل على أجهزة الكومبيوتر.

جاك (off screen)
فينا نشرب قهوة؟

صوفيا (off screen)
ليه؟

جاك(off screen)
بدي إحكي معك

تسود لحظة صمتٍ محرجة.

جاك (off screen)
بليز، عم أُطلبا منّك.

جاك وصوفيا جالسان في زاوية في أقصى المقهى. جاك يحتسي قهوته، بينما تنهي صوفيا آخر جرعة من كأس النبيذ.

صوفيا
متر، بليز بعد واحد.

جاك
هيدا الثالث!

صوفيا
غير إنّه تسألني عن صحتي وأمي وشغلي. ليه جبتني لهون؟

جاك
هون كنّا نلتقى دايماً، هون شربنا أوّل فنجان قهوة سوا.

صوفيا
بعرف! أنا ما وقّفت إجي عليه. بس إنت، هلّق تذكّرته؟!

جاك متردّد، لا يعرف من أين يبدأ بالحديث.

صوفيا
جاك؟

جاك
بعدِك بتحبّيني؟

صوفيا

تأخذ وقتها

ما بعرف.

جاك
ما بتعرفي. مين بيعرف؟!

صوفيا
ما بعرف مين بيعرف! ليه إنت بتعرف؟!

جاك
إيه بعرف!

صوفيا
تجوّزنا وشفنا.

جاك
شو شفتي؟

صوفيا
أديش كنت موجود!

جاك
أنا؟ ليه وين كنت عم روح؟!

صوفيا
إذا بتنلقح بوجي عالكنباية مش معناتا إنك معي!
إنت بعيييد عني، كتير بعيد! ولا كأنك حاسس فيي، صفر مشاعر.
بترجع عالبيت بآخر الليل، ما بدّك تحكي ولا تسمع شي، راسك
عم يوجعك، وبدّك تشرب بيرتك لتروق!

جاك
بكون راجع مطووش من الشغل!

صوفيا
ونهار السبت عندك الدكتوراه.
على راسي، ما حدا بيقدّر طموحك قدّي. بالعكس هيدا
يمكن واحد من الأسباب إنّي حبيتك.

إيام الأحد كنت إترجّاك لنروح شي محل، «تعبان»
و«شوب»، كل النهار بوجّ التلفزيون، «تيك، تيك، تيك، تيك»

صوفيا تقلّد حركته في الضغط على جهاز التحكم بالتلفزيون عن بُعد.

لعّيبة الفوتبول تبع الدرجة الثالثة بتعرف أساميهن!

جاك

طيّب الأحد هو النهار الوحيد اللي بقدر مدّ إجريي!
بيطلعلي إرتاح أنا كمان! جلديني صوفيا، جلديني!

هنا يبدأ الضغط بالارتفاع.

صوفيا

أنـا عـم إجلدك؟! مدري مين عـم يجلد التاني!
لمـا اضطريـت نـزّل الـ bébé ، فكّرت تجي معـي؟! كنت حاملة
إبـن الجيـران ببطني ما هيك؟!

جاك

إمّك راحت معك. شو بدنا نروح نعمل كلنا هونيك؟!

صوفيا

ما بدّي إمّي معي أنا! بدّي اياك إنت حدّي.
عندي رجّال أو ما عندي؟!

جاك

لأ عندِك رجّال صوفيا! بس لو تسمعيله وقت بيحكي، يمكن ما كان
مات الولد أصلاً!
«يا صوفيا روقي، يا صوفيا ارتاحي»! انحشرتي تفتحي ورشة البيت
وتركضي وراء شغّيلة العمار إنت وحبلة!»

صوفيا

الشاليه الزريبة اللي كنت معيّشنا فيه بلا ولد وما كان سايعنا!
وين بنيّم الولد؟ ووين بضبلّه غراضه؟ قلّي! بس يمكن لو
حضرتك ساعدتني ببرغي واحد بهالبيت، ما كان مات البيبي!

جاك

لأنّه فاضي راضي أنا، معلّا إجريي كل النهار! ما عندي شغل!

صوفيا

مش وحدك جاك، أنا كمان بشتغل، وبروح عالسوبرماركت
وبحضّر أكل، وعملت الورشة!

صوفيا تصمت للحظة.

خلص جاك! تعبت نتشارع، عن جد تعبت. منّا على نفس الموجة.
أفضل إذا كل واحد بيرجع يعمل حياتو مع الشخص المناسب.

المشهد ٣٧
منزل ويليام، غرفة النوم

موسيقى «بوسانوڤا» برازيلية تصدر عن جهاز الفينيل. ويليام مستلقياً على السرير، يمارس تمرين الشهيق والزفير في جهاز قياس التنفس[٢]، حيث ترتفع كرة بلاستيكية زرقاء صغيرة وتسقط، ثم تعود للارتفاع بحسب تنفّس ويليام. جاك يقف بجانبه.

جاك
خلّي الطابة فوق قد ما فيك، ريّح، رجاع نفوخ عن جديد.
لازم تعملا عطول هيدي، بتفتحلك نفسك وبتريّحك.

ويليام
بدّا فحمة.

جاك بالكاد يبتسم.

جاك
أحسن اليوم، عم تتنشّط مرّة عن مرّة.

ويليام
كتير منيح. وين السهرة؟

جاك يتظاهر بالابتسام مرّة أخرى.

ويليام
دخلك باك شي؟ مثل اللي ناسيينن بلا دفن!

جاك
ضهرت مع حدا!

ويليام
خاي خاي انبسطلّا، بس مين هيدي؟!

جاك
صوفيا، مرتي. طلع في رجّال تاني.

ويليام
أوف!

ويليام يجمد للحظة.

كيف عرفت؟

٢ في لبنان، يُطلَق عليه إسم «الأركيلة».

Flashback

المشهد ٣٨

مقهى جاك وصوفيا المفضّل

جاك

... الشخص المناسب؟!

ما تكوني ملاقيتيه كمان لهالشخص المناسب؟

تهز رأسها نفياً.

جاك

أكيد؟!

جاك يحدق في صوفيا، محاولاً قراءة مشاعرها.

عيونك بقولوا غير هيك!

صوفيا

ما عندي حدا ثاني.

صوفيا تتحدث بهدوء، رغم أنها منغمسة في أفكارها المشتتة.

بس ضهرت مع حدا.

جاك

ضهرتي مع حدا!!

صوفيا تهز رأسها إيجاباً.

جاك

ونمتي معه؟

صوفيا ترفع نظرها وكأنها تستجدي الصبر الإلهي.

جاك

شو؟!

صوفيا

هيدا همّك؟!

جاك

جاوبي!

يزداد التوتر بينهما.

صوفيا

شو بيقدّم وبأخّر معك؟!

جاك
بيقدّم وبأخّر كتير!

صوفيا
إلنا أربع أشهر تاركين، بلّشنا معاملات الطلاق، وأنا وإنت مش قادرين نتّفق عا لون الماي. شو بأثر معك إذا نمت ولّا ما نمت؟!

جاك
أكتر ما بتتصوّري!
بعدنا ما طلّقنا، ولمعلوماتك إنت بعدك مسجّلة على إسمي!

صوفيا
مسجّلة!! على إسمك! ما تكون مفكرني سيارة أنا!! مسجّلة على إسمه! وما زالك هيك إي نمت معه. وانبسطت كمان!

صوفيا تأخذ حقيبتها لتغادر.

وبليز بكرا الصبح بتمضي أوراق الطلاق وما بتقلّي «بدّي فكّر»، أصلاً ما كتير بيلبقلك تفكّر.

صوفيا تغادر المقهى. جاك يضرب الطاولة بقبضة يده غضباً.

Flashback ends

الكرة البلاستيكية الزرقاء الصغيرة لا تزال ترتفع ثم تسقط، ثم ترتفع من جديد.

هذه المرّة، جاك هو المستلقي على السرير، ينفخ في جهاز قياس التنفس يائساً.

ويليام يقف بجانبه مع ابتسامة مرحة على وجهه، يربت على كتف جاك متعاطفاً معه.

ويليام
كمان نفخة... بتريحك هيدي.

جاك
آآآآه!

ويليام
نفوخ نفوخ، بترتاح

جاك
قولك بيعرفني؟

ويليام

بنبرةٍ ساخرة.

طبعاً. وعاملّه مسّاج كمان.
يا رجل ليه عم تشغّل راسك بهالأشياء؟!

جاك
بشو بدّك شغّل راسي؟! كم بيضة بحطّوا بالغاتو؟!
عم قلّك مرتي نامت مع واحد تاني!

ويليام
بس ما انتو تاركين وعم تطلقو.
يعني ما غشّتك.

جاك
تركِت البيت بس بعدا مرتي.

ويليام
عالورق.

جاك
بعدا مرتي!!!

تنتهي أغنية وتبدأ أغنية جديدة من نوع البوسا نوفا:
"Você vai ver"*.

ويليام
خلّينا نتفّق على شغلة: مرتك سبق وخسرتا، يعني قصتك قصّة ego!

جاك
ليك، صاروا كذا مرّة بدّي قلّك ياها وبرجع بسكت. بس هلّق خلص رح بقّا للبحصة.
بتعرف شو أكتر شي بكرهه؟ العالم اللي بصيروا ينظّروا وهنّي مش دايقين الشغلة، عم يتفرّجوا من برّا! إنت شاطر تقرط حكي!
عيش مع مرا قبل وبعدين تبقى وعظني.

ويليام
وإنتَ ملك الهروب للأمام. بس يفتحلك الواحد موضوع شوي دقيق، دغري بتقوّص عليه.

جاك
وإنت ملك التنظير.

ويليام
يمكن. بس مش أنا اللي عندي مشكل مع مرتي.
جاك، إنت بتسمع بس ما بتتسمّع.
سؤال: مرتك شلكّة شي؟!

جاك لا يجيب.

برأيك شو صار لوصلت لهون؟!

جاك لا يجيب.

سألتك قبل وعم إرجع إسألك، ليه بتحبّا؟

جاك لا يجيب.

جاك؟

جاك
بعتذر بس ما باخد دروس بالزواج من واحد متفرّج.

ويليام
هلّق ضروري كون شيف مع نجمة ميشلان لأعرف طعمة تمّي؟!

جاك

مدندناً أغنية داليدا

Paroles, paroles, paroles[٣]

ويليام
مش يمكن لإنه قدّ ما بعرف شو هو الزواج، ما تزوّجت؟!

جاك
Paroles, paroles, paroles[٤]

ويليام يصمت للحظة، ويتأمل في أرجاء الغرفة وفي المكتبة التي تحتوي رفوفها على أسطوانات الفينيل القديمة.
بعد لحظات، ويليام يقرّر أن يروي لجاك قصته.

ويليام
أحلى مرا بالعالم، التقيت فيا بقبرص...

flashback

المشهد ٢٩
مدخل فندق في قبرص، ليلاً

تصل إلى مدخل الفندق دراجة صغيرة من نوع «سوزوكي لاندي» وعلى متنها أربعة أشخاص متلاصقين.
يقود الدراجة رجل، وتجلس خلفه فتاة، وويليام (٣٧ عاماً) يجلس على المسندة المعدنية الخلفية، وخلفه الدكتور فؤاد معلقاً في

٤ Blah, Blah, blah

الهواء، يداه على خصر ويليام الذي يُمسكه من ساقيه. جميعهم ثملون ويصرخون بعبارة «إيلا ري»[٥].

تتوقّف الدراجة، يترجّلُ منها ويليام مرتدياً بدلة بدون ربطة عنق.

ويليام
بعد كاس.

السائق
ولا نقطة.

ويليام
بشرفكن!

الفتاة
باي ويلي.

تنطلق الدراجة.

د. فؤاد

(صارخاً)

إيلا ري

ويليام
إيلا ري

الباقون
إيلا ري

ويليام
إيلا ري

ويليام يخرج إلى تراس الفندق. المكان شبه فارغ باستثناء طاولة واحدة. عازف البيانو يعزف لحن أغنية «Você vai ver».

يوجد على البار جواز سفر برازيلي، وكتاب، وكأس من الشمبانيا. الساقي منهمك بتحضير مشروب.

عند وصول ويليام، يبتسم الساقي له ويتحدث معه بالإنجليزية مع لكنة قبرصية.

ويليام
إيلا ري

بارتندر
إيلا ري

٥ «إيلا ري» هي عبارة يونانية تُستخدم لإلقاء التحية.

ويليام

Scotch please (سكوتش، لو سمحت)

بارتندر

Here you go sir (تفضّل)

ويليام

Got a match? (بلاقي معك ولّاعة؟)

بارتندر

Sorry, Sir

ويليام

بار أوتيل ما في ولعة! إي والله لو منّا كنتوا بعدكن عالحمير.

ويليام يأخذ رشفة من مشروبه ويلتفت ليرى من يوجد في الحانة. يجول بنظره في أرجاء المكان، يمرّ على عازف البيانو، ثم يلتفت وينظر مجدداً بسرعة كما لو أن شيئاً غير اعتيادي لفت انتباهه.

يركّز جيداً، يرى امرأة مستلقية على الأرض تحت البيانو الطويل. ينظر ويليام، وهو يشعر بالثمالة، إلى كأسه، يرمش بعينيه، ثم ينظر مجدداً تحت البيانو. المرأة لا تزال هناك.

ويليام

Do you see things under the piano or is it the whiskey?!

(شايف شي تحت البيانو أوهيدا مفعول الويسكس؟!)

بارتندر

(مشيراً إلى الباسبور البرازيلي وكأس الشامبانيا على البار)

There is a lady over there. **(مبلا في مرا هونيك.)**

ويليام

Interesting! **(مش قليل!)**

ويليام يتوجه صوب البيانو وينحني ليكلّمها.
ميوتشا (٣٢ سنة، مختلطة الأعراق وغير تقليدية) مغمضة عينيها ومفتونة بالموسيقى.

ويليام

Hello

ميوتشا

(تفتح عينيها)

Hi

ويليام

How's the weather there? **(كيف حال الطقس عندك؟)**

ميوتشا
(تفضّل وشوف.) Come check it out for yourself.

ويليام يتردد للحظة، ثم يستلقي بجانبها تحت البيانو.

ويليام
Any chance for rain so you hid here?
(معقول تشتي فتخبّيتي هون؟)

ميوتشا
(عم إتسمّع عالموسيقى.) I was just listening to the music.

ويليام
What's wrong with listening from over there?
(meaning the bar)
(وشو المشكل إذا تسمّعتي من هونيك؟ (يقصد البار))

ميوتشا
Just close your eyes and let it in.
(غمّض عيونك وأتـرك حالك)

ويليام يغمض عينيه ويستمع. تبدو على وجهه علامات التأثّر.
يفتح عينيه.

ويليام
واو!

ميوتشا
You feel the sound vibrations with your body.
It impacts you both emotionally and physically.
It's proven to reduce stress and anxiety.
(بتحسّ بالذبذبات الصوتية بجسمك. بتأثّر عليك عاطفياً وجسدياً،
ثبت إنه هالشي بيخفّف التوتر والإنكزايتي)

ويليام
True!
(عن جد!)

ويليام ينظر إلى قدمَي عازف البيانو وخصره فوقهما مباشرة.

ويليام
Let's hope that this guy didn't have beans for lunch.
(بتأمّل الشب ما يكون آكل فاصوليا عالغدا.)

ميوتشا تنظر إليه وينفجر كلاهما من الضحك.

Flashback ends

جاك

(ضاحكاً)

تحت البيانو؟

ويليام
تحت البيانو!

جاك
شو قلتلّي إسما؟

Flashback continues

ويليام وميوتشا جالسين على مقعديهما على البار.

ويليام
William

ميوتشا
Miuca (ميوتشا)

ويليام
Miuca! Interesting name. (ميوتشا! إسم مميز.)

ميوتشا
It's Brazilian. (إسم برازيلي.)

الساقي
Sorry, we're closing. (بعتذر منكن بس عم نسكّر البار)

ويليام يستاء من الساقي ويتحدث إليه باللغة اللبنانية.

ويليام
هلأ صرت بدك تسكّر يا شرموط؟!

الساقي
Excuse me? (عفواً؟)

ويليام

(مبتسماً له)

Thank you لحاس طيزي.

الساقي
Has tizi?!

ويليام
Yeah, it's Lebanese brown pudding, you'll love it.
(نعم، هيدي أكلة حلو لبنانية لونا بني، رح تعشقا)

الساقي
.Nice (آه، لذيذ.)

ويليام وميوتشا يغادران الحانة القريبة من الشاطئ.

ويليام
Let's walk (منتمشّى شوي)

ميوتشا تشير إلى فستانها وإلى كعبها العالي

ميوتشا
!Perfect outfit (تيابي روعة لهيك شي!)

ويليام يركع أمامها، يرفع قدمها، ويخلع فردة من حذائها بينما ينظر في عينيها. ميوتشا تتفاجأ في البداية، ثم تبتسم وترمي رجلها الثانية في الهواء خالعة الفردة الثانية التي تتطاير في الهواء.

ويليام يقفز من الحافة إلى الرّمل، ويمد يده لمساعدتها. ميوتشا تتشبّث به وتقفز.

يُسمَع رنين خلوي.

Flashback ends

جاك يبحث في جيبه عن هاتفه الذي يرن ويأخذ المكالمة.

جاك
إيلا ري سلوى؟ قصدي إي سلوى؟... يلّا مشوار الطريق.

جاك يُنهي المكالمة.

جاك
تأخّرت عا موعدي.

جاك ينهض ليغادر.

ويليام
عم تحكيا؟

جاك
ما عم تردّ عليّي! آخر جلسة كانت كتير عاطلة.

ويليام
مين غير إنتو التنين عنده مصلحة ترجعوا سوا؟

جاك يستوعب ما يلمّح إليه ويليام.

المشهد ٣٠
منزل جيهان (والدة صوفيا)

صوفيا وجيهان تتشاجران.

جيهان
...وقلتلّو يجي يتعشّى عنّا. وين المشكل؟! جاك شب طموح وإبن عيلة، عندو أغلاطو؟ دبش؟ الرجال كلّن هيك صوفيا. أوعا تفكّري رح تلاقي واحد كامل.

صوفيا
ماما، ما بريدِك تدّخّلي!

جيهان
ضلّيتي تقوليلي ما تدّخّلي لوصلتي لهون!
إذا هلّق ما بدّي جرّب أعمل شي. أيمتى؟!

صوفيا
يا ريت جرّبتي تعملي شي بعلاقتك مع بيّي، بدل ما توعظيني لإلي!
ولّا كنتي عم بتفتشي على الرجّال الكامل إنتي كمان!!

جيهان
مش وقته هالجدل صوفيا ليه فلّ بيّك!
بس بالقليلة أنا تزوّجت عشر سنين. عملت ولد.وجرّبت كثير!
انتي شو لحّقتي تشوفي من الزواج؟! ما طبقتي السنتين وعم تطلقي!

صوفيا
عم إتعلّم منك ماما. مش أحسن ما إجني على ولد وخلّيه يربى بلا بي؟!

جيهان تتفاجأ بكلمات صوفيا القاسية. صوفيا تتأسّف لما قالته، لحظات وتقترب من أمها وتأخذ يدها.

صوفيا
عفواً ماما، ما قصدي.

صوفيا تفكّر للحظة.

خلص، منتعشّى.

المشهد ٣١
منزل ويليام

ويليام وطوني جالسين إلى جانب المسبح.

طوني
...التغت الصفقة مع الصينيين. بعتوا جواب رسمي إنّن ما رح يفوتوا.

ويليام
طبيعي. الإستاذ جميل عمل كل شي ليهشّلن، وهشلوا.

طوني
بس ما عم إفهم شو هدفه. ما هو كمان عندو أسهم بالشركة. وكان قاتل حاله يبيع!

ويليام
طوني حبيبي، هلّق تغيّرت المعطيات. بكرا أنا بروح بس أسهمي بيبقوا هون. رح ينطرحوا بالمزاد وأعضاء مجلس الإدارة عندن الأولوية. أيا حمار بعلّيلن قيمتن قبل ما يشتريهن؟!

طوني
وشو ناوي تعمل؟!

ويليام
صراحة ضايع بين الأبيض والأسود.

طوني
ما فهمت!

ويليام
لون التابوت. شو قَولك؟ الأسود بيعطي فخامة ما هيك؟

طوني
بعتذر، وبعرف إنو حديث ثقيل بس هَي الشركة يا ويليام فيا أكتر من ٢٠٠ موظّف وعيلة بعيشوا منّا!!

ويليام
قولك الأسود لمّيع أو ناشف بيطلع أحلى؟

Cut to

المشهد ٣٢
مكتب تصميم داخلي

صوفيا تعمل على أحد الملفات. تتوقف وتحدق في الباقة التي بدأت أوراقها تذبل.

بعد لحظة تأمل، تتوجه إلى خزانة الملفات، تفتحها وتبحث فيها حتى تجد ملف ويليام.

تبحث عن رقم هاتفه الأرضي، وتتصل به.

مدبرة المنزل
Good morning (بونجور)

صوفيا
Hello, is Mr William here?
(آلو، موسيو ويليام موجود؟)

مدبرة المنزل
Who's this please? (مين طالبه؟)

صوفيا
A friend. (صديقة)

مدبرة المنزل
Sorry ma'am, I need a name please.
(بعتذر مدام، بس بدي إسم.)

صوفيا
Never mind. (خلص معليه.)

صوفيا تنهي المكالمة، ثوان وتحمل حقيبتها وتغادر المكتب.

Cut back

جاك يصل الى منزل ويليام مرتدياً سروال سباحة وتي-شيرت، حاملاً حقيبة أكبر من العادة.

جاك
Bonjourno (بونجورنو)

طوني
مرحبا

ويليام
مكبّر الشنطة مبيّن؟!

جاك
محضّرلك مفاجأة.

ويليام
مخبّالي فيا مرا حلوة؟

طوني
طيّب أنا بستأذن.

ويليام
طوني بتتذكّر كنت ضل قلّك «time is money»؟ (الوقت ثمين)
إنسَ. Time is priceless، (الوقت ما بيثمّن)
روح عمول شي بتحبّه.

طوني وعلى وجهه تبدو ملامح التعاطف والإحباط معاً، يقف ويغادر.
ويليام يتوه في أفكاره المظلمة.
جاك يحاول تلطيف الأجواء، فيخلع قميصه ويُخرجُ أوزان
الستايروفوم من حقيبته، ويغطس في حوض السباحة.

جاك
اليوم التمرين بالماي، لالالاا!.

جاك يقوم بحركة تمرين مائية.

ويليام
ما رح إنزل بالماي.

جاك
ليه؟

ويليام يهزّ رأسه رافضاً.

جاك
بس أنا عندي خبريّة كتير حلوة.

ويليام
خبّرا عاليابسة.

جاك
شو باك دخلَك اليوم! بدّا تجيك؟!

ويليام
هيك شي.

جاك
إذا هيك بلا ما تسبح، بتلوّنا أحمر.

ويليام

(ضاحكاً)

Pas Mal!
منّك هيّن!

جاك
شو إنت وحدك بدّك تضيّفني لبن؟!

ويليام

خي، شكلك مبسوط اليوم.

جاك

بشرفَك ما تزَعّلني. ما تنزل بالماي. قعود عالحافّة، منسولف
ومنخبّر خبار وإذا بدّك بلا التمرين.
بس مش بالأوضة، بتطربقلي عا قلبي.

ويليام يحدّق في وجه جاك للحظة، ثم يذهب ويجلس على حافة حوض السباحة، ساقاه في الماء.

ويليام

تفضّل.

جاك

Nooo. Age before beauty! (لاااا، العمر قبل الجمال!)

ويليام

يمكن age أنا، بس إنت من وينلك البيوتي؟!

جاك

انت بتغار منّي.

ويليام يضحك.

نزلتوا تتمشّوا عالبحر، وبعدين؟

ويليام

أيّ بحر؟!

جاك

لك الإيلا ري.

ويليام

فاتح مدرسة للولاد أنا! خبّرن قصص قبل النوم.

ويليام يقرر أخيراً أن يكمل قصة ميوتشا.

جاك

في حدا يعملنا بوشار؟

صارخاً.

ماتيو، اثنين بوشار ملح زيادة.

ويليام يضحك.

flashback

المشهد ٣٣
شاطئ رملي، ليلاً

ويليام وميوتشا يسيران على الشاطئ، مياه البحر تلامس أرجلهما، وعلى مسافة بعيدة منهما، ثمة مجموعة من الأشخاص المتحلّقين حول نارٍ مُضرَمة.

ويليام
What brings a Brazilian girl to Cyprus?
(شو جاب بنت برازيلية على قبرص؟)

ميوتشا
A wedding. You? (عرس، وأنت؟)

ويليام
Meetings. (إجتماعات.)

ميوتشا
What do you do? (شو بتشتغل؟)

ويليام
Investments and funds mainly.
(الاستثمارات والتمويلات، بشكل أساسي.)

ميوتشا
Oh, a golden boy. (آه، الفتى الذهبي)

ويليام

ويليام يضحك.

Yes. You? (إذا بدك، وأنتِ؟)

ميوتشا
I'm not as shiny as you. I'm an artist.
(أنا أرتيست. ما بلمّع مثلك)

ويليام
Ouch! Where I come from, "Artist"is the legal term for prostitutes. You have to be more specific.
(من وين إنا جايي كلمة «أرتيست» هي التعبير القانوني للعاهرات. فا لازم تكوني أدقّ من هيك.)

ميوتشا
تضحك
A painter, I paint. (رسّامة، برسم.)

ويليام
Nice. What do you paint? (حلو! شو بترسمي؟)

ميوتشا

My emotions. (مشاعري.)

ويليام

And you have a lot of them I bet.
(وما بعرف ليه عندي إحساس إنن كتار)

ميوتشا

And very mixed ones. (وكتيييير متضاربين)

ويليام

Schizophrenic, Bipolar!
Like I love you for breakfast and hate you for lunch.
(انفصام بالشخصية، بايبولير! من نوع الـ «بحبك على الترويقة بس بكرهك عالغدا»)

يضحكان. يقتربان من مجموعة عُشّاقٍ يجلسون حول النار ويشوون النقانق والمارشميلو. توجد حولهم كميات كبيرة من زجاجات البيرة الفارغة الملقاة على الرمال.

فتاة ١

Beauty is relative... (الجمال نسبي...)

شاب ١

(بلكنة إيطالية)

Beauty is mama mia (الجمال mamma mia)

شاب٢

My turn, my turn. The word is love, you start
(صار دوري، صار دوري. الكلمة هي «الحب»، تفضّلي.)

فتاة ٢

Oh, let's see. Love, is, Eh...Many splendid things?
(أوه، هات لنشوف. الحب هو...مجموعة إشياء حلوة مخلوطة ببعضا؟)

شاب ١

Love is a voluntary prison. (الحب هو حبس تلقائي.)

الفتاة ٢ وهي حبيبة الشاب ١ رميه بحبة مارشميلو بعدما سمعت إجابته.
ويليام وميوتشا يصلان حيث توجد المجموعة.

ويليام

إيلا ري.

شاب ١

إيلا ري.

الشاب ٢ يقدم لكل منهما سيخاً من حلوى المارشميلو، ويليام وميوتشا يأخذانها.

ويليام

Thank you

(شكراً)

شاب ٢

مخاطباً ميوتشا

What's your definition of love? (شو مفهومك للحب؟)

ميوتشا تستغرب السؤال وتتردد.

شاب ٢

We're playing a game. Come on.

(عم نلعب لعبة، لازم تجاوبي.)

ميوتشا

Love, Eh... A Miracle?

(الحب، ممممم.... معجزة؟)

شاب١

Bella Bella. (شو حلو، شو حلو!)

الرجل ١ يرسل إلى ميوتشا قبلة في الهواء.
الجميع ينظر إلى ويليام منتظراً جوابه.

ويليام

(ينظر إلى ميوتشا)

Love?... Well, I haven't been there yet but I intend to have a good answer by morning.

(الحب؟... لهلّق ما عندي فكرة بس حاسس إنه من هون للصبح رح يكون عندي الجواب.)

عند ما يستوعبون إعلان ويليام ولعه بميوتشا، يبدأون بالتصفيق والصفير ويقف الشاب ١ ويرفع ذراع ويليام عالياً معلناً فوزه.

شاب ١

Campione, campione.

(بطلنا لليلة، بطلنا.)

Flashback ends

ويليام لا يزال جالساً على حافة الحوض. جاك داخل الحوض يُحرِك ساقَي ويليام.

جاك
أيواا...الحبّ لما يفرقع!

ويليام
إي واللّه. بحياتي ما احترقت عا مرا هيك!

ويليام يقرر التجاوب ويبدأ بتنفيذ التمرينات تلقائياً. جاك يصحح حركاته، وويليام يتبع تعليماته.

جاك
واكتشفت الحبّ ما علينا؟!

ويليام
شو بقول المثل؟ يضرب الحبّ شو بذلّ؟

جاك يضحك. وليام مطبطباً على صدره.

أنا هو! كانوا عم يحكوا عني أنا...

flashback

المشهد ٣٤
فندق في قبرص عند الفجر

يفتح باب المصعد في أحد طوابق الفندق، ويخرج منه كلٌّ من ويليام وميوتشا.يسيران في الممرّ إلى أن تصل ميوتشا إلى باب غرفتها. تعيد له سترته التي كان قد وضعها على كتفيها ليقيها من البرد.

ويليام
So what do we do now?
(وهلأ شو العمل؟)

ميوتشا
Sleeping is good for your skin.
(النوم مفيد لبشرتك.)

ويليام يضحك. من النافذة تدخل أولى خيوط الشمس.

ويليام
فيي طلّعك عاأوضتي؟ بوّسلك أصابيع إجريكي واحد واحد؟

ميوتشا
What did you say?
(شو قلت؟)

ويليام
عم قول إنو عبالي فصفصِك. سامعة بالبروستد؟
بدّي فصفصك مثل البروستد.

ميوتشا

Well not tonight. (مش الليلة.)

ويليام

But I'm leaving tomorrow and ---!!!
(بس أنا طاير بكرا، و... !!!)

ويليام يستوعب أنها فهمت ماذا قال وأجابته عندما تكلم معها بالعربية. يقف مسمّراً عينيه جاحظتين وكأن ماء مثلجة وقعت عليه. ويليام الذي يشعر بالحرج الشديد لدرجة أنه يعجز عن التكلم، يقوم بإيماءات مشيراً إلى أنها فهمت ما قاله، ثم يشير الى جواز سفرها البرازيلي، محاولاً استيعاب كيف أنها تلاعبت به طوال السهرة. يلطم جبهته بنعومة على الحائط.

ويليام

ما إلك حق... ما إلك حق. والباسبور البرازيلي وإسمك!؟

ميوتشا

تضحك

نص الشعب البرازيلي من أصل لبناني.

ويليام يضع يداً على عينيه من شدة الإحراج بينما يضرب الحائط باليد الأخرى.

Flashback ends

جاك يضحك عالياً.

جاك

آخخخ...آخخخ يا خواصري! ما بقا فيي! دخيلكن!

ويليام

مبسوط إي؟! عم سلّيك.

جاك

روعة! أهضم خبريّة بالعالم!

ويليام

إي والله، إذا بدّي ألّفا ما بتزبط هيك!
إنت خبّرني، شو النبأ السارّ؟

جاك

رايِح إتعشّى عندا بكرا عشيّة.

ويليام
أوف! كيف ركّبتا؟

جاك
جايتك الخبريّة بس خلّينا نغطّسلك راسك شوي بالماي أحسن ما تاكلا ضربة شمس.

ويليام ينظر ثانية إلى جاك قبل أن يقرّر النزول إلى الماء.
يقف ويليام في الحوض، ثمّ يغمّس رأسه في الماء.رأس ويليام تحت الماء وعيناه مفتوحتان. في الجانب البعيد من حوض السباحة، يرى امرأتين. إحداهما في أوائل الستينيات من عمرها والأخرى في منتصف الأربعينيات، تنظران إليه.ويليام يهلع ويخرج رأسه من الماء بسرعة وهو في حالة ذعر شديد، ساعلاً ولاهثاً .

جاك
شو في، شو صار؟!

ويليام يتمسّك بحافّة الحوض محاولاً استعادة أنفاسه.

جاك
ويليام؟!

ويليام
ما شي، خلص، خلّيني إرتاح شوي.

في هذه الأثناء، تصل صوفيا بسيارتها وتركنها على مسافة من منزل ويليام. تخرج من السيارة وتتجه نحو البوابة الرئيسية.
ويليام ممدد على الكنبة وفي مقابله يجلس جاك. ماتيو يمسك بكوبٍ من الماء.
ويليام الذي أصبح في حالٍ أفضل.يلفت انتباهه شيء ما على شاشة هاتفه. بهدوء، يلقي نظرة فاحصة. شكوكه كانت صحيحة.

عبر كاميرات نظام الأمان الموصول الى هاتفه يتأكد أنها صوفيا التي تقف عند المدخل!

ويليام
وين صافف؟

جاك
تحت الأرض. ليه عم تسأل؟

ويليام
لا، قلت بتمشى معك عالسيارة، بدي إحكيك شوي.

ويليام يشير إلى ماتيو لكي يقترب منه.

ماتيو؟

ماتيو يقترب منه. ويليام يهمس بضع كلمات في أذنه.ماتيو يغادر على الفور.

صالون المنزل مؤلف من واجهات زجاجية تسمح برؤية داخله من الحديقة.
ماتيو يسير مع صوفيا في الفناء الخلفي متأكداً أن ظهرها للصالون، يناور بمهارة لاهيا إياها بالحديث من أجل تشتيت انتباهها.
في نفس الوقت، ينهض ويليام ويصطحب جاك إلى سيارته، متبادلاً معه أطراف الحديث ومتأكداً أن يكون ظهر جاك للحديقة تفادياً لرؤية صوفيا.
بأعجوبة، تصل صوفيا ويغادر جاك دون أن يلتقيا.

ماتيـو وصوفيا على الشـرفة. ماتيـو يدعو صوفيا إلى الجلوس.

صوفيا
وحضرتك اشتريت البيت؟

ماتيو
نعم

صوفيا
من قديش هيدي؟

ماتيو
شي شهرين.

صوفيا
وما بتعرف شي عنه؟

ماتيو
أنا اشتريت بواسطة شركة عقارية. ما التقينا ولا مرّة.

صوفيا التي تجول بنظرها في أرجاء المكان تلحظ وجود ساعة «أوديمار بيغه» على طاولة القهوة.

صوفيا
ولمّا باعك البيت باعك ساعته معه؟!

ماتيو
لأ هيدي ساعتي.

صوفيا
ساعتك؟ غريب لإنّا مثل ساعته تمام!

ماتيو
آه والله؟! الهيئة عنا نفس الذوق، حبّيته.

ماتيو يفكّر للحظة.

شو عاملة عشيّة؟ فيي إعزمك عالعشا؟

تتحرّك كاميرا المراقبة المعلّقة في السقف فوقهما.

في غرفة النوم، ويليام مستلقياً على سريره يشاهد المشهد بأكمله على هاتفه من خلال تطبيق كاميرا المراقبة.

ويليام يداعب وجه صوفيا على الشاشة بأصبعه.

المشهد ٣٥

قارب صيد عند المغيب

ندي وجاك على متن القارب الراسي في البحر، يحتسيان البيرة، وأمامهما صنارتا الصيد. ندي يكتب رسائل نصية على هاتفه.

جاك

...أثقل شي بشغله لربيع إنّه ما في وقت.
صار حالة طارئة اضطر يلغي الصيد.

ندي يتكلّم مع جاك بينما يتابع حديثه على تطبيق واتساب. يُصدر هاتفه صوتاً ينبهه إلى أن البطارية سوف تفرغ تماماً.

ندي

نزّلتلّي دمعتي! بكون عملّو شي ألف دولار هلّق! مشّينا!

جاك

فيك تشيل هالتلفون من إيدَك. قرّفتني!

ندي

روق! عم يحكوني شغل من الصّين!

في نفس اللحظة، تفرغ بطّارية هاتفه.

ندي

لأ، لأ، لأ!

جاك

شو في؟!

ندي

خلصت بطّاريتي وما معي شاحن!

جاك

منيح هيك ارتحنا!!... أنا نازل عالحمّام.

جاك يتوجه إلى الطابق السّفلي.
على الفور، ندي يأخذ صنارة جاك ويبدأ بسحبِها بسرعة.

Cut to

المشهد ٣٦
منزل ويليام

ويليام في غرفته يقرأ كتاباً. يتعب من القراءة، يمسك بصورة فوتوغرافية لأرجوحة شبكيّة فارغة من على الطاولة القريبة منه، ويضعها داخل الكتاب كعلامة مرجعية.

على أحد الرفوف أمامه توجد صورة فوتوغرافية داخل إطار فضي. ويليام يحدق بها. الصورة هي للمرأتين اللتين شاهدهما في قاع المسبح.

Cut back

جاك
منمشي؟ ما بدّي إتأخّر عالعشا.

ندي
أوكي

ندي يبدأ بسحب صنارته. وجاك يفعل بالمثل، إلّا أنّه يشعر بثقل غير عادي في صنّارته.

جاك
ندي، ندي، في شي كبير علقان!

ندي
شو عم تحكي؟!

جاك
اووووو! مش عم فيّي شدّا قد ما تقيلة!

ندي
تمسّك فيا منيح. سنود إجرَك بالحفة. إي سندا مزبوط!

جاك يضع رجله على حافّة القارب ويميل نحو الخلف بينما يلفّ حبل الصنارة بيده.

جاك
أنا بقول تونا. على أطيب أكلة سمك، فيا كيف ما كان عشرين كيلو!

جاك يغنّي محتفلاً.

وزّع شوكولاتا وطعمينا، وزّع شوكولاتا وطعمينا.

جاك يمسك أخيراً بالفريسة، فيتفاجأ بأنها مجرد لعبة ضخمة من القماش على شكل سمكة محشوّة بالأثقال.
جاك يحدّق في اللعبة مندهشاً، غير قادر بعد على استيعاب ما حدث.

ندي الذي دبّر المقلب لجاك، ينفجر مقهقهاً على أرض القارب.
جاك يستوعب ما فعله ندي، فيبدأ بضربه، بينما ندي لا يتوقّف عن الضحك. جاك ينفجر من الضحك هو الآخر.

جاك
حيوان! أقسم باللّهحيوان!

ندي
آخ يا خواصري آخ...رح موت.

جاك
إذا بتلاقي أكمخ منك بتنتحر! طيّب يلّا، خلصنا هرقة، مشّينا.

ندي ينهض وهو لا زال يضحك، ويتوجّه نحو مقود القارب. يحاول تشغيل المحرّك، لكنه لا يعمل.

Cut to

المشهد ٣٧
منزل جيهان، ليلاً

جيهان تشاهد التلفزيون. تخرج صوفيا لتجد أمها في هذه الوضعية. فتتوقف للحظة تتأملها، قبل أن تلاحظها جيهان.

جيهان
ريحة بتشق القلب! شو حاطّة بالفرن؟

صوفيا
كيش فيتا وزعتر برّي، أكلته المفضلة.

جيهان تبتسم مسرورةً عندما تسمع أن صوفيا حضّرت طبق جاك المفضل.

صوفيا
رح فوت أعمل دوش وغيّر ثيابي.

Cut back

ندي في القارب يحاول الاتصال بخفر السواحل طلباً للمساعدة، بينما يجلس جاك في الخلف محبطاً وحزيناً.

ندي

بان، بان، جميع السفن، جميع السفن. هون قارب «النسيم» على بُعد ميل ونص بحري غرب «رأس طبرجا»، تعطل الموتور ونحن بحاجة لمساعدة سحب. قارب «النسيم»، انتهى.

جاك

مش عا أساس صلّحت المارش؟! ...هات، اعطيني هالتلفون لقلّن إنّي مأخّر. إجري بحظّي!

جاك يحدّق في أرضية القارب يائساً، متسائلاً كيف له أن يخبر صوفيا بأنه سيتأخّر على الموعد. ندي الذي لا يزال يتواصل مع خفر السواحل، يمسك بهاتف جاك ويلقيه إليه. جاك غافل وغير متنبّه، لا يلتقط الهاتف، فيقع في الماء.
صوت ارتطام الهاتف بالماء يوقظ جاك ويعيده إلى الواقع.

جاك

ندي، مش وقت مزحاتك، واصلة معي لهون!

ندي

لك هيدا تلفونك!!

جاك

ندي، ما عم إمزَح، فيني إقتُل زلمي هلّق!

ندي يشعل مصباح يديوي، ويركض كالمجنون نحو حافة القارب ليبحث عن الهاتف في الماء.

ندي

لك هيدا تلفونك مش عم إمزَح!

جاك يدرك أخيراً أنها ليست مزحة من مزحات ندي المعتادة. فيلتقط شبكة صيد صغيرة ويمرّرها في الماء في محاولةٍ يائسة لالتقاط الهاتف.

جاك

كم مرّة صرت قايلّك ما تكبّ التلفون!

ندي

وإنت بتقلّي كبّه وما بتطلّع!

جاك

أنا قلتلّك كبّه يا كذاب؟! أنا قلت مرّقه!

جاك يفقد صوابه، فيهجم على ندي غاضباً ويضع يديه على عنقه وكأنه سوف يخنقه.

المشهد ٣٨
منزل جيهان، ليلاً

صوفيا في المطبخ، ترتدي ملابس بسيطة وإنما أنيقة، تغسل الأطباق، وإلى جانبها تقف والدتها جيهان التي تقوم بتجفيفها.
وبينما تعملان في صمت، يقرع جرس الباب.
صوفيا لا تبدي أي رد فعل، جيهان تذهب لتفتح الباب.
إنه جاك، لا يزال مرتدياً ملابس البحر، ويحمل في يده كيس هدية.

جاك
sorry، بس إنقطع الـ boat فينا بالبحر ووقع تلفوني بالماي!

جيهان لا تجيب.

جاك
بعرف إنّك بتكرهيني.

جيهان
أنا بكره شوف صوفيا زعلانة.

جاك
فيّي إحكيا؟

جيهان
يحيّي بالمطبخ.

جاك يتوجّه نحو المطبخ.

جيهان
بتعرف جاك، كتير هيِّن الرجّال يرضي مرا، إذا قرّر.

جاك يهزّ رأسه تقديراً لما قالته، ويتابع طريقه.

في المطبخ، جاك واقفاً خلف صوفيا يراقبها، بينما هي تتابع جلي الصحون دون أن تلتفت إليه.

جاك
ما رح أعطي حجج على الأرجح ما رح تصدّقيا.
بس بدي قلّك
إنه ما في محل كنت بفضّل كون فيه الليلة، أكتر من إنّه كون هون عم إتعشّى معك.

جاك يقترب من صوفيا ويطبع قبلة على رأسها من الخلف بينما تتابع عملها.

جاك
بعتذر!

جاك يصفن قليلاً.

في حدا قلّي إنّه أنا بس بسمع لجاوب، مش لإستوعب شو عم يجرّب يوصلّي الشخص اللي بوجّي. ولقيت إنه معه حق.

صوفيا
من أنا و زغيرة كنت ضلني ناطرة بيّي يجي. كل ما شوف طيّارة قول أكيد هو فيا.
وشفت إمّي كيف عملت كل شي لوحدا. وانتهت لوحدا.

صوفيا تتنهّد وكأن ثقل العالم يجثم على صدرها.

وما عبالي عيش نفس الشي.

جاك
sorry، ما انتبهت لهالشي من قبل. كنت ملتهي كتير بحالي.

جاك يأخذ علبة صغيرة من الكيس الذي يحمله، يفتحها، ويضعها على طاولة المطبخ. في العلبة سوار من الذهب المرصع بحبوب ألماسٍ صغيرة على شكل كلمة «Love».جاك يغادر.

المشهد ٣٩
سيارة جاك

جاك جالس في سيارته عند إشارة مرور حمراء في زحمة النهار. يرن هاتفه.

إنها رسالة واتساب صوتية من مديره نبيل.

نبيل (عبر الرسالة الصوتية)
«هاي جاك، مروق عليي على المكتب قبل ما تبلّش شغل عاوزك بموضوع.»

المشهد ٤٠
مكتب نبيل

جاك يصل متحمّساً وسعيداً. يطرق باب مكتب نبيل (٤٥ عاماً)، و يدخل.

نبيل
قعود.

جاك يجلس.

نبيل
كيفك؟

جاك
روعة.

ممازحاً.

ما بدي ياك تعتل همّ شـي. إنت بس طلاع بالطيارة وفلّ، وأوعك ترجع.

نبيل
تغيّر القرار، جاك!

جاك
أيّ قرار؟!

نبيل
الإدارة فضَلت تختار شخص تاني ليكون رئيس القسم.

جاك
شخص تاني؟! مثل مين يعني؟!

نبيل
جان بروڤو

جاك
جان! أكيد عم تمزح معي. هلّق جان صار أشطر مني؟!

نبيل
جاك، إنت بتعرف رأيي بالموضوع!

جاك
لأ ما بعرف. بعرف إنه جان ما معه شهاداتي ولا خبرتي. هلكوا عيوني وخسرت زواجي لعملت هالدكتورا عا نصيحتك. وهلّق بتقلّي جان هو للي رح يصير رئيس القسم!

نبيل
الفرنساويي بيملكوا أكثرية المستشفى جاك!

بعد لحظاتٍ قليلة من الصمت، جاك ينهض ويخلع روبه الأبيض.

نبيل
شو عم تعمل؟!

جاك
برفض إشتغل تحت إيد واحد بيفهم أقل مني.

نبيل
جاك بلا خوات. إنت بتعرف وضع المستشفيات وإنه المراكز المهمة مأخودة.

جاك
ما رح موت من الجوع.
عندي عيادتي الخاصة، وزواج بالعناية الفايقة بدّو إنعاش!

جاك يغادر.

نبيل
جاك... جاك...

المشهد ٤١
منزل ويليام

ويليام مستلقياً بملابس السباحة على كرسي للاسترخاء، يقرأ كتاباً. ماتيو ممدّد على مقعد تمارين رياضية، يمارس تمارين ضغط الصدر تحت قضيب رفع الأثقال.
كلما رفع الأثقال، يصدر أصواتاً غريبة وكأنها خارجة من أحشائه.
الصوت يشتّت تركيز ويليام، الذي ينظر إلى ماتيو مندهشاً.

ويليام
يا إبني إنت شو عم تمرّن بالضبط، مصارين؟!

ماتيو ينفجر من الضحك عندما يسمع التشبيه، ويفقد قوته على رفع قضيب الأثقال، فيعلق تحته.

ويليام
تسؤ، تسؤ، تسؤ! يا حسرتي!

ماتيو
بليز ويليام، مش أنا وعم إتمرّن!

ويليام
تتمرّن؟! إذا مش شايفك الواحد شو عم تعمل، بفكّرك عم تستفرِغ!

ماتيو يضحك من جديد. في هذه الأثناء، يصل جاك ويضع حقيبته على الأرض، ويساعد ماتيو على التخلّص من الأوزان.

ماتيو
Mais il est fou, il veut me tuer!
(مجنون، بدو يقتلني!)

جاك في حالة مزاجية سيئة، يجلس على كرسيٍ إلى جانب ويليام.

ويليام
شو في بتضلّك مطنبز؟!

ماتيو
عن جد! مين طمبوزو؟!

ويليام وماتيو يضحكان.

جاك
عم سلّيكن إي؟!

ويليام
شو في اليوم؟!

جاك
بعدين

جاك يلحظ صورة الأرجوحة الشبكية التي يستعملها ويليام كعلامة مرجعية للكتاب. جاك يمسك الصورة ويتمعّن فيها عن قُرب، ويرى الأرجوحة معلّقة في حديقة خضراء بين شجرتين. يبدو المنظر في الصورة جذاباً ومريحاً.

جاك
شو عبالي كون بآخر الدني، ملقوح عا واحد متل هيدا!

ويليام
وصوفيا معربطة فيك؟

جاك ينظر إلى ويليام دون أن يجيب.

Flashback

المشهد ٤٢
منزل ميوتشا القروي، نهاراً

* اغنية *"Colour me in" لداميان رايس تسمع في الخلفية.

أرجوحة شبكية معلّقة بين شجرتين، هي نفسها التي تظهر في صورة ويليام. ويليام وميوتشا مسترخيان في الأرجوحة. كلاهما عاريان، لا يغطيهما سوى شرشف خفيف. ويليام يداعب خصلة من شعرها. وعلى خصر ميوتشا علبة من حلوى الشوكولاتة. يأخذ ويليام واحدة منها.

ويليام
شو سرّ الشوكولا بعد السكس؟

ميوتشا
ناقصك حنان حياتي.

ويليام يضحك، ويقدم لميوتشا قطعة شوكولاتة، ولكنها ترفضها.

ويليام
عم تقوليلي لأ!؟

ميوتشا
مممم... إي

ويليام
بتعرفي آخر وحدة قالتلي لأ عا شوكولا شو صار فيا؟!

ميوتشا
شو صار فيا؟!

ويليام
نزل وزنا.

ميوتشا تضحك.

ويليام
ما رح وقّف إغراءات لتاخدي بعد.

ميوتشا
ما تتعّب حالك. وما تكون مفكّر حالك كثير مغري يعني.

ويليام يضع قطعة شوكولاتة في فمه ويتذوّقها متظاهراً الشعور بالألم من شدة النشوة. بعد الانتهاء من مسرحيته، يرمقها بنظرة إلّا أنها تصرُّ على عدم الاستسلام لإغراءاته.ويليام يأخذ قطعة أخرى من العلبة ويمسكها بين إبهامه وسبابته.

ويليام
هيدي الكرة الأرضية، أنا نايم هون

مشيراً إلى نقطة محددة في قطعة الحلوى.

وإنتي لاقطّيا بين إصبعين، وقادرة تَعملي فيا اللي بدّك.
بتقدري تفعصيا إذا بدك.

ميوتشا
وين قلتلّي إنت؟

ويليام
هون.

يشير مجدداً إلى النقطة.بشغف وشهوانية، تقضم ميوتشا قطعة الشوكولاتة، ومعها برفقٍ أصبع ويليام. تضحك.

ويليام
أي!!!

يثبتها وينظر في عينيها للحظات ثم يقبلها بحرارة وتندلع بينهما جولة حب جديدة.

Cut to

أغنية *"Colour me in" لداميان رايس ما زالت تسمع في الخلفية.
ليلاً، ويليام وميوتشا لا يزالان مستلقيَين في الأرجوحة الشبكية، يغطيهما شرشف خفيف.
القمر المكتمل وبعض الشموع المبعثرة على الأرض تكفي لإضاءة المكان.

ويليام يقرأ من كتاب بصوتٍ مرتفع.

Cut to

في اليوم التالي، داخل منزل قروي صغير ساحر، لوحات فنية منثورة في أرجاء المكان.ويليام يجلس على كنبة ساكناً في وضعية جانبية. يمسك بيده الممدودة مكنسة من الطراز القديم. يرتدي بنطالاً كتانياً وقميصاً أزرق سماوياً مفتوح الأزرار، وقد أسقط أعلاه ليكشف عن أحد كتفيه. ميوتشا ترتدي قميصا أبيض فضفاضاً، تقف أمامه، مواجهة لوحة قماشية موضوعة على منصبٍ ثلاثي القوائم، ترسم شيئاً لا يراه ويليام.

ويليام
انشالّله اليوم!

ميوتشا
طالعة بتعقّد!

ويليام
نمّلت إيدي. بعدين شو الفكرة من المكنسة؟!

ميوتشا
يا ذكي المكنسة بس للوضعية، بالآخر برسم غير شي محلّها.

بعد لحظات.

ويليام
خلص!!

ميتوشا
لأ! ما تقوم.

ينهض ويليام من مكانه ويرمي بالمكنسة أرضاً، ويبدأ بتحريك يده ليتخلّص من حالة الخَدَر التي أصابته.

ويليام
رح إقتل حالي!

ويليام يتجه نحو اللوحة ليرى ما رسمته ميوتشا.
ميوتشا تبتعد نحو الكنبة وتبدأ بالضحك. ويليام ينظر إلى اللوحة فيرى أنها لا تمت له بصلةٍ نهائياً. إذ يرى بورتريه لفتاة كانت ميوتشا تنسخها من صورة جواز سفر مثبتة في أعلى المنصب ثلاثيّ القوائم.

ويليام
شو هاي؟! وين صورتي؟!

ميوتشا تضحك وتحتمي خلف الكنبة.

ميوتشا
بقلبي.

ويليام يدرك أنه كان مقلباً من ميوتشا، فتتأرجح ردة فعله بين الضحك والعصبية.

ويليام
بدّي إقبعلك إياه لقلبك!

ويليام يبدأ بملاحقة ميوتشا حول الكنبة.ميوتشا تنفجر من الضحك بينما تهرب منه راكضةً حول الكنبة.

ويليام
ياي شو رح يصير فيكي!

ويليام يمسك بالمكنسة ويوجهها نحو ميوتشا مهدداً إياها.

ويليام
مكنسة إي؟ بدّي مشّطلك شعرك بالمكنسة!

ويليام يبدأ بمطاردتها مرة أخرى. ميوتشا وفرشاة الرسم بيدها تهدده بها.

ميوتشا
عا وجّك!

يحاول ويليام القفز فوق الكنبة ليلحق بها، لكنها تسبقه بضربة من الفرشاة التي ترسم بها حرف «M» على قميصه ووجهه. ويليام ينظر في المرآة ليرى ما فعلته، فيزيد تصميمه على الإمساك بها.

ميوتشا تبدأ بالضحك والصراخ، فتُسقِط فرشاة الرسم من يدها وتهرع إلى الحديقة، ثم تلقي بنفسها في الأرجوحة الشبكية.

ميوتشا

Sorry, sorry William!

ويليام

شو بعمُل فيكي؟ هم؟

يقبّلها لثوان بينما يستلقيان في وضعية معاكسة لطول الأرجوحة. ميوتشا تضحك.

ويليام

ما تتحرّكي.

يختفي ويليام لبضع ثوانٍ ثم يعود حاملاً منصَباً ثلاثي القوائم في أعلاه كاميرا. يوجهها نحو الأرجوحة ويضبط المؤقت.

ويليام

بتعرفي إنه ما عنّا ولا صورة سوا! غير اللّي بقلبك!

ويليام يركض مسرعاً نحو الأرجوحة.

زيحيلي، زيحيلي.

يصل ويُلقي بنفسه إلى جانب ميوتشا، فتنقلب فيهما الأرجوحة ويقعان على الأرض بينما يضحكان ويصرخان.تتمايل الأرجوحة فارغة. الكاميرا تلتقط صورة الأرجوحة الفارغة.

Flashback ends

المشهد ٤٣

مكتب تصميم داخلي

صوفيا تصل إلى مكتبها فتتفاجأ بوجود باقة كبيرة من الورود الحمراء الجميلة. تتأمّل الباقة وتجد عليها بطاقة دُوِّنَت عليها جملة بخط جاك: «ما بدّي عيش بلاكي».

المشهد ٤٤

منزل ويليام

ويليام وجاك يمارسان التمارين المائية في حوض السباحة. إلى جانبهما، ماتيو مسترخياً في الماء. ويليام يمسك بالأثقال الرغويّة ويرفعها إلى الأعلى بناء على تعليمات جاك.

جاك
جمّد كوعك بزاوية تسعين درجة. وبروم معصمك شمال، يمين، شمال، يمين...

جاك يساعد ويليام على تنفيذ الحركة بشكل صحيح.

جاك
...غنّي «Frère Jacques»

ويليام يرمي بأحد الأثقال الرغويّة في وجه جاك، ويضحكان.

ويليام
وأخيراً حكيتوا، مش تشارعتوا. هيّي فتحتلك قلبا، وإنت، إنت شغلة كبيرة. بلّشت تفهم اللغّة.

جاك
تلميذك.

ويليام
بس هلّق لازم تكمّل. ضروب الحديد هو وحامي.
فكّر بشي كانت صوفيا تحبّه، وانت ما كنت تسايرا فيه.

جاك

يحاول جاهداً البحث عن إجابة.

أوف... ساعدا بعفش البيت.

ويليام
طيّب ليه يا ربّي ليه؟! شو عامِلّك أنا؟! جاك؟! عفش؟!

جاك
أوكي أوكي... الرقص، كتير بتحب تروح عشي محل ترقص.

ويليام
شكراً، فيك تعرفلنا وين سهرانة هالويك أند مثلاً؟

جاك
رايحة على Effy's

ويليام يتفاجأ من معلومات جاك الدقيقة وإجابته السريعة.

جاك
شو؟! أصحاب مشتركين سهرانين معاً. هنّي خبّروني.

ماتيو
Il faut absolument que tu changes de look bébé.
(بس كتير ضروري تغيّر ستيلك حياتي!) MAKEOVER!!!

جاك
ليش شو بهن تيابي؟ ما بلبس حلو؟!

ويليام وماتيو ينظران إلى بعضهما وينفجران من الضحك.

جاك
شو هالمنايك!

ويليام
بعدين المرا رايحة لهونيك لترقص. فإذن بدّك ترقّصا.

جاك
رقّصا؟! خلّيا تبلّش تقولّي «مرحبا» أول شي.

ويليام
إنت ركّزلي عالرقص وتروك الباقي عليّ. بس لما قول ترقّصا يعني ترقّصا. بطريقة تخلّيها تتذكر ريحتك!

جاك
تتذكّر ريحتي!

ويليام
كيفَك بالرقص؟

جاك
تمام

ويليام
ما بعرف ليش قلبي مش متطّمن.

ويليام ينظر إلى ماتيو الذي يهزّ رأسه موافقاً.

ويليام
فرجينا

جاك
مشّوني يا شباب.

ويليام
فرجينا!

جاك
شو بابور! هه!

جاك يقوم بأداء بضع حركات راقصة.
ويليام وماتيو ينظران إلى بعضهما من جديد و ينفجران من الضحك. جاك يغضب ويبدأ بضربهما بينما يضحكان.

جاك
حلّو عني أنا فالل!

ماتيو يستوقف جاك ويمسكه من خصره بإحكام.
جاك يتفاعل مصدوماً من لقطة ماتيو.

ماتيو
بتلقطا هيك.

جاك يحاول الفرار من قبضة ماتيو، لكن ويليام قد أطبق عليه من الخلف وأمسك به من خصره هو الآخر. جاك يجد نفسه محشوراً بين الاثنين «كالسندويش».

ويليام
هيك بتذكّرا بريحتك!

ماتيو
١, ٢, ٣, ٤... ١, ٢, ٣, ٤...

ماتيو يكرّر خطوات الرقص أكثر من مرّة لكي يتقنها جاك العالق بينهما. خلال تأديتهم للحركات الراقصة، تخرج مدبرة المنزل إلى الشرفة متوجهة نحوهم.

عندما يلاحظون وجودها، ينفصلون بلحظة عن بعضهم البعض بطريقةٍ مضحكة وكأن شيئاً لم يحدث: ماتيو يرفع نظره إلى السماء، جاك يبدأ بالصفير، ويليام يغوص تحت الماء.
في الطرف البعيد من الحوض، يرى من جديد المرأتين اللتين رآهما سابقاً. يراهما تبتسمان له وتشيران إليه ليقترب منهما. ويليام الذي لم يهلع هذه المرّة، يستمر في النظر إليهما، إلى أن تسحبه يدي جاك خارج مياه الحوض.

جاك
باك شي؟!

ويليام يهزّ رأسه نافياً.

المشهد ٤٥
غرفة نوم ويليام

ويليام يجري اتصال فيديو مع جاك الذي يتحضّر للذهاب إلى السهرة.

ويليام
...غيّر القميص.

جاك
ليه؟!

ويليام
لأنو ما إلَك حق تلبس قميص منقّط مع جاكيت مقلّمة. حطّ شي سادة. يلاّ لشوف!

جاك
أوكي، أوكي!

جاك يبدأ بخلع القميص.

بس معقول فوت عالمحل مثل القطشة؟!

ويليام
انت وصال عالبار وارتاح.
شو رح تشرب الليلة؟

جاك
شو بعرّفني. شي قنينة بيرة أو Bloody Mary

ويليام
إلهي لماذا تركتني؟! مشروب لونه أحمر جاك!
سكوتش يا ولد، بتشرب سكوتش مع ثلجتين!

المشهد ٤٦
ملهى ليلي

كأس فارغ على البار يُلقى بداخله مكعبان من الثلج، ثم يُسكب بعض الويسكي. يُقدم الساقي المشروب لجاك الجالس إلى البار. يأخذ جاك رشفةً ويُبدي استياءه من مذاقه.

تقترب امرأةٌ مثيرةٌ في منتصف الأربعينيات من عمرها من البار وتكلّم الساقي.

صولانج
كاس متله بليز.

صولانج (٤٥ عاماً) تجلس بجانب جاك وتضع يدها على فخذه..

صولانج
هاي يا حلو!

جاك
إنتي مين؟!

صولانج
أنا الطُّعم.

جاك
طُعم شو؟!

صولانج

اللي بتحطّه بالصنّارة لتعلق السمكة. قالولي بتحب الصيد.
شكله ما خبّرَك ويليام!

جاك

يخبّرني شو؟!

صولانج

مبتسمة

ألف باء الانجذاب إذا بدّك.
أنا هون لأكّد إنّك رح تحلى بعين مرتك الليلة.

جاك

إجري بمرتي، بدّي كمّل حياتي معك وجيب منّك سبع ولاد!

صولانج

تضحك مجدداً.

تأخرت شوي حياتي.

في هذه اللحظة، تصل صوفيا مع أصدقائها، يخلعون معاطفهم، ويجلسون إلى طاولتهم. فجأةً، إحدى صديقات صوفيا تدفعها بمرفقها بقوة، بحيث تكاد تفقد توازنها.

صوفيا

شو صرلك؟!

صديقة صوفيا

البار! اتطلّعي بس بلا ما تطلّعي!

صوفيا تتفاجأ لرؤية جاك متأنقاً وصولانج بجانبه.
تلتقي نظراتهما، جاك يرفع كأسه لها.

Cut to

الملهى امتلأ بالناس والسهرة في أوجّها...

صوفيا

معقول ملّا وحدة معو؟ قد سِتُّه!

صديقة صوفيا

حياتي الرجال هيك! عالعشرين بدُّن واحدة بالأربعين. وعلى الأربعين بيركضو ورا العشرين.

يقترب النادل من طاولة صوفيا حاملاً زجاجة «Moet» وردية وكؤوس شمبانيا فارغة.

على البار، صولانج تضع يدها على رقبة جاك، الذي تبدو عليه الدهشة.

صولانج
قلّي شي.

جاك
شي؟!

صولانج
شو ما كان. ركّب تلات كلمات على بعض.

جاك
ما عم إفهم عليكي!

صولانج تضحك ضحكةً مجلجلة، متظاهرةً بأنها تستمتع بوقتها إلى أقصى حد. النادل يُعلِم صوفيا أن زجاجة الشمبانيا هي تقدمة من جاك.صوفيا تنظر نحوه فترى المشهد المصطنع والمُدبّر من صولانج.

صولانج
طيّب حياتي، صار وقت أنا فوت عالحمام وإغرق بالبلّوعة.

جاك
خلّيكي، ما تفلّي.

صولانج

تقرصه من خدّه.

حياتي نحنا بدنا نولّعلك ياها للأمّورة، مش نفجّرا!

صولانج تأخذ حقيبتها وتغادر.
في هذه الأثناء، يضيء هاتف جاك، تصله رسالة واتساب من ويليام.

ويليام
Try to be funny. (جرّب تكون مهضوم.)
وما تنسى المجاملات والحكي المعسول.

Cut to

صوفيا، ثملة بعض الشيء، تتمايل مع الموسيقى.
في اللحظة المؤاتية، يظهر جاك خلف صوفيا وهي ترقص، ويضع يديه على خصرها. تستسلم صوفيا للحظة، لكنها لا تلبث أن تحاول الإفلات من قبضته.جاك الواقف خلفها يُحكم قبضة ذراعيه حولها الى ان تستسلم.

صوفيا
بعّد عني، روح عند صاحبتك.

جاك
غرتي؟

صوفيا
هاهاهاها إي كتير.

جاك
هيدي مريضتي، إجت تسلّم عليي.

صوفيا
آآآه! مريضتك! بأي وضعية كانت تحتّى فكّت رقبتا؟

جاك
اشتقتلك

جاك يهمس في أذن صوفيا وهو يضمُّ جسدها إلى جسده ويتمايلان على أنغام الموسيقى. جاك يحني رأسه نحوها فتلامس أنفاسه رقبتها.

جاك
اشتقت لريحتك

صوفيا تحاول مقاومته لكن دون جدوى. تخذلها أحاسيسها.

صوفيا
إنت واحد حمار

جاك
وانتي كتير حلوة

صوفيا تغمض عينيها، وتسلّم نفسها له وللموسيقى.

المشهد ٤٧
منزل ويليام

الغرفة خافتة الإضاءة. ويليام يسعل بشكل متكرّر. تصله رسالة على هاتفه. يتفقّده، إنها صورة لجاك وصوفيا يرقصان ويتعانقان. يضع الهاتف جانباً. سُعال ويليام يزداد سوءاً. نراه يغرق في أفكاره المظلمة، وتبدو عليه ملامح القلق والخوف.

ويليام
حكي معي... حكي معي...

بيأس، ويليام يدفع بيده كل ما على الطاولة التي بجانبه فتقع الأغراض أرضاً...
يفتح الجارور المجاور له ويخرج منه حقنة وبعضاً من المورفين. يملأ الحقنة من القارورة، يشد الرباط حول ذراعه، ويحقن نفسه بالإبرة.

Cut back

...جاك يُدير صوفيا نحوه بحزمٍ ليصبحا وجهاً لوجه.

جاك
ما بدّي عيش بلاكي!

ويقفان هناك للحظات، ينظر كل منهما في عيني الآخر.

Cut to

المشهد ٤٨
منزل جاك وصوفيا

يُفتَح باب المدخل. جاك وصوفيا يقبّلان بعضهما بشغفٍ بينما يعريّان بعضهما من الملابس. يعلق بنطال جاك حول كاحليه فيتعثّر ويجرّ صوفيا معه. يرتطمان بأثاث المنزل قبل أن يسقطا على الكنبة ضاحكين...

في صباح اليوم التالي في السرير، تستيقظ صوفيا من النوم وتفتح عينيها. تفكّر للحظة قبل أن تستوعب أين هي.
جاك مستلقياً بجانبها، كان يتأملها وهي نائمة، يبتسم لها.

جاك
صباح الخير.

صوفيا تبادله الابتسامة على الرغم من الأسئلة الكثيرة التي تدور في رأسها.

جاك
صباح النور.

يقترب ويطبع قبلة على شفتيها.

جاك
صباح الفلّ.
قهوة؟

صوفيا

بليز.

جاك ينهض من السرير ويتوجه إلى المطبخ. صوفيا لا تزال تتذكّر وتستوعب ما حدث الليلة الماضية. يرنّ هاتف جاك الموضوع على طاولة السرير بجانب صوفيا.

صوفيا تنزعج من رنينه المتكرر فتضغط على زرّ الصامت دون أن تُركز جيّداً على هوية المتصل.

لحظة وتُلقي نظرة ثانية على الهاتف. ترمش من دهشتها. إنها صورة ويليام.

صوفيا

ألو... ألو...

لا أحد يُجيب وينقطع الاتصال. في هذه اللحظة، يدخل جاك مع القهوة.

جاك

مين؟

صوفيا

تبدأ بالارتجاف

ليه ويليام عم يدقّلك؟!

جاك

ويليام مريض عندي.

صوفيا

مريض؟!

جاك

عندو كانسر وعم إهتمّ في.

صوفيا

ويليام معو كانسر!!

جاك

إي...إنتِ من وين بتعرفيه؟!

صوفيا مصعوقة، ينعقد لسانها وتعجز عن الكلام.

جاك

صوفيا؟!

المشهد ٤٩
منزل ويليام

جاك في سيارته يصل بسرعة جنونية الى منزل ويليام. يركن سيارته في منتصف الطريق ويترجّل منها مسرعاً تاركاً بابه مفتوحاً.

يضغط على جرس المنزل بشكل هستيري، ثم يطرق الباب عدّة مرّات إلى أن تحضر مدبرة المنزل وتفتح له الباب.

تفتح مدبرة المنزل الباب، فيدفعها جاك بغضب شديد ويدخل. ماتيو جالس في غرفة الجلوس.

جاك
وينه؟!

جاك يتوجه نحو غرفة ويليام ويقتحمها كالوحش الكاسر. ويليام في سريره يسعل، شاحبٌ وعليل. جاك يمسكه من قميصه.

جاك
يا حيوان. يا بلا أخلاق. عامل حالك صاحبي. وين نمت معا؟ عا هيدا التخت؟ بالبيسين؟ مطرح ما بمرّنك وبهتم فيك؟ وين؟!!

ماتيو يدخل الغرفة مسرعاً ويهرع إلى إبعاد جاك عن ويليام، ويطرحه أرضاً. سُعال ويليام يشتدّ ويتأزّم.

ماتيو
Tu es fou ou quoi ? (مجنون إنت؟!)

جاك يحاول النهوض، لكن ماتيو يثبته بقوة من رقبته بحركة تكاد تخنقه.

ماتيو
إذا بتقرّب عليه بقتلك!

يحمرّ وجه جاك من قبضة ماتيو حول عنقه.

ويليام
تركه، ماتيو تركه!

ماتيو
بتروق وبتحكي متل العالم؟

جاك الذي يكاد يختنق يهزّ رأسه موافقاً. ماتيو يفلت جاك ليدعه يتنفّس، ويعطيه بعضاً من الماء. جاك يشرب.

ويليام
تركنا شوي.

ماتيو
No Way (أبداً)

ويليام
ماتيو!

ماتيو يذعن لأمر ويليام، وعند مغادرته يلتفت نحو جاك.

ماتيو
Je te promets, je te tue. (بوعدك بقتلك) إذا بتقرّب صوبه.

ويليام في سريره، بينما جاك لا يزال ممداً على الأرض.
ويليام متفاخراً.

ويليام
نامت عندك إيه؟!

جاك
مبسوط عم تتسلّى فينا!

ويليام
كلنا في حدا عم يتسلّى فينا! أنا من ٥ أشهر كنت بطل العالم....
قلت بركي إذا برجّعكن لبعض...

جاك
كان لازم تخبّرني!

ويليام
خبّرك شو؟!
«هاي جاك، أنا ويليام ونايم مع مرتك»

جاك
شو بلا أخلاق!

ويليام
كنتو عم تطلّقوا، وكان في يكون حايلّا شخص ثاني.

جاك
بتضلّك بلا أخلاق!

ويليام
أوكي أنا بلا أخلاق. بس بدّك تضلّك عامل الضحيّة ولّا بدّك شي مرة تفوت بصلب الموضوع؟! ليه وصلتوا لهون؟

جاك يرفع أصبعه الوسطى في وجه ويليام.

ويليام
برافو! هيدا الشاطِر فيه. بس ما تبكي.
دخلك شفتك هيدي عم ترجف ولّا أنا غلطان؟

جاك
في سبب إنّك ملقوح بهالتّخت. بتعرف شو هو؟ إنه في الله!

ويليام
وتارك واحد متلك يتزوّج مرا متل صوفيا؟؟!

جاك
ما تجيب سيرتا عا لسانك!

في هذه اللحظة، يبدأ ويليام بالنظر إلى سقف الغرفة متجاهلًا ردود فعل جاك، وكأنه يقول: «بتعرف شو؟ إنسَ، متّك خرج الواحد يضيّع وقته عليك».

جاك
بآخرتك ملقوح لوحدك هون بالتخت! متل الصرصور!
ولا عايلة، ولا ميوتشا؟! وينا؟ إي وينا؟ ولاّ عرفتك على حقيقتك؟!

ويليام لا يجيب، ويكتفي بالنظر إلى جاك باستحقار واستهتار.

جاك
أنا رح قلّك ليه إنت لوحدك: لإنك واحد مأيّر! فهمت؟ مأيّر!

ويليام
وعبالك تعرف قديش؟!

flashback

المشهد ٥٠
فندق قبرص، المغيب

على الشاطئ الرملي في نفس الفندق الذي التقى فيه ويليام وميوتشا للمرة الأولى، يقف كلّ من رئيس بلدية لارنكا، وميوتشا مرتدية الأبيض، وصيفتها، والدكتور فؤاد. جميعهم ينتظرون وصول ويليام.

تنظر ميوتشا إلى فؤاد وكأنها تسأله: «أين هو؟!»
ؤاد يهز رأسه ويرفع كتفيه وكأنه يقول «لا أدري».
صل ويليام وهو يغني. من الواضح أنه كان يشرب الكحول.
يُقبّل ميوتشا.

ميوتشا
كنت عم تشرب؟

ويليام
Un poquito.
(شوي)

رئيس البلدية
Ok. Let's do this.
(خلّونا نباشر!)

Cut to

Two hours earlier

ويليام واقف أمام النافذة الزجاجية لغرفته في الفندق، سارحاً في أفكاره. يرتدي بنطالًا إكرو أبيض اللون وقميصاً أبيض. طرقات على الباب تقطع حبل أفكاره.

ويليام

Come in. (تفضّل)

يدخل موظف خدمة الغرف ومعه سترة البدلة لون إكرو أبيض، يسلمها إلى ويليام.

خدمة الغرف

Your jacket sir. (الجاكيت، موسيو.)

ويليام

Thank you. (شكراً.)

يغادر موظف خدمة الغرف.

أمام المرآة، ويليام يرتدي سترته ثم يحدق في نفسه تائهاً.

المشهد ٥١

حانة الفندق

وليام يصل إلى الحانة لتناول مشروب.

ويليام

Tequila please. (تيكيلا إذا بتريد.)

يستدير الساقي. إنه نفس الرجل الذي كان خلف البار عندما التقى بميوتشا للمرة الأولى.

الساقي

Hey! "Has tizi man" (هاي، رجل «الهاس تيزي»)

ويليام

مبتسماً

Yeah. Has tizi big time. (إيه والله، لحاس طيزي عالآخر!)

يسكب له الساقي قدحاً من التيكيلا.في مواجهة ويليام، تجلس شابّتان مثيرتان ترمقانه وتبتسمان له.

ويليام يرفع لهما قدح التيكيلا قبل أن يتجرّعه.

Cut back

يُسمَع خطاب رئيس بلدية لارنكا بطريقة متقطّعة ومبعثرة.كما لو أن الكلمات عن فكرة الألتزام تضرب دماغ ويليام كالمطرقة.

رئيس البلدية

Your life will change... There is no more "you", only "us"
Sacrifices, sacrifices, sacrifices...
Forever, ever, ever...

(حياتك سوف تتغير...) (من الآن فصاعداً، لم يعد هناك «أنت»، بل فقط «نحن»...) (تضحيات، تضحيات، تضحيات...)
(إلى الأبد، أبد، أبد...)

Cut to

An hour earlier

وليام والشابتان المثيرتان والساقي يشربون ويتقهقهون.يهمُّ الساقي إلى سكب جولة أخرى من أقداح التيكيلا، لكن ويليام يقلب كأسه.

ويليام

No no no! (لا لا لا!)

الشابة ١

Come on! (مبلا يلاّ!)

ويليام

I have a wedding to attend. (عندي عرس.)

الشابة ٢

Seriously?! Is this thing still legal?!
(عن جد؟! بعدو قانوني هالشي؟!)

يضحكون.

الشابة ١

Come to our room. We have weed!
(تعا لعنّا عالأوضة، عنّا ماريوانا.)

ويليام

Ciao ladies. (باي صبايا.)

Cut to

ويليام في حمام لوبي الفندق يرشّ وجهه بالماء.ينظر إلى المرآة ويتحدث إلى نفسه، محاولاً النطق بكلمة «نعم».

ويليام
نـع ... نعـ .... نع....بدّك تقبل! رح تقبل!

ويليام يصفع نفسه مرة ثم مرتين. يشير بإصبعه نحو المرآة مهدداً نفسه.

ويليام
بتقبل!

Cut back

ويليام وميوتشا أمام رئيس البلدية

رئيس البلدية
Please, face each other, hold each other's hands, and repeat after me:
(إذا بتريدوا اتطلّعوا ببعض، امسكوا إيدين بعض، وعيدوا ورايي)

ميوتشا وويليام يكرران خطاب قسم الزواج بعد رئيس البلدية. مع التقدم في الخطاب، يخفت صوت ويليام تدريجياً حتى يصلا الى مرحلة الموافقة. ميوتشا: «نعم، أوافق».ويليام لا يقوى على قولها. الجميع يحدّقون به، بينما هو شارد تماماً وكأنه خارج جسمه.

مع عودته تدريجياً إلى الواقع، ينظر إلى عيني ميوتشا بشغف وحب، ثم يقبّلها.

ويليام
بحبك كتير. كتير!

ثم يستدير وينطلق مغادراً، تاركاً الجميع في حالة من الذهول.

Flashback ends

المشهد ٥٢
منزل ويليام

جاك متأملاً ويليام باشمئزاز.

ويليام
قرفان؟!

جاك
شو مأيّر!

ويليام
عأساس الحياة اللي عيّشتا إنت لمرتك بعد الزواج قمّة الخوجنة ما هيك؟!

جاك
عالقليلي بعدني معا!

ويليام

ويليام يرمق جاك بنظرة تشاوف.

تكرم، تعا كل يوم.

جاك
عالقليلة في رجّال حدّا، مش واحد جبان، بيهرب وقت الجد!

.يطرق ماتيو الباب ويدخل

ماتيو
ويليام، وصل موعدك.

ويليام
يلاّ.

يقترب ماتيو لمساعدته على النهوض.
أثناء خروجه من الغرفة، يتوقّف ويليام ويستدير نحو جاك.

اللي صار صار، وما كان كتير حلو. بس إنت بتقرر إذا بدّك تضلّك مفوكس عالنص الفاضي من الكبّاية أو تركّز عالنص المليان.
Adiós (وداعاً)

Cut to

على سطيحة المنزل ويليام والدكتور عمر يتناولان الفطور.

د. عمر
أنا آسف ما جيت زرتك قبل. بس صراحة ما هان عليّي شوفك هيك ويليام، إنت شيخ الشباب.

ويليام
طال عمرك دكتور. أكيد الوزارة لاهيتك كثير. أنا كمان كنت بفضّل ما تشوفني هيك. وبشكرك إنّك لبّيت دعوتي بسرعة.

د. عمر
طلبك غالي.

ويليام
كتير منيح. إنت بتعرف قديش بتسوى شركتي.

د. عمر
أكيد.

ويليام
أنا بملك ٤٥ بالميّة منّا.
حصتي بدّي إتبرّع فيا لمركز السرطان اللي إنت مأسّسه.

د. عمر
آه هاه!

ويليام
وعندي أمنية وحدة.

المشهد ٥٣
ملهى ليلي

جاك يجلس إلى البار وحيداً، مكسوراً وثملاً. ينهي مشروبه في جرعة واحدة ويغادر.

جاك يتجوّل في الشوارع، تائهاً ويائساً.

المشهد ٥٤
منزل ويليام

ويليام مستلقياً على أريكته المفضلة وهو يقرأ كتاباً.
يرن جرس الباب، وبعد لحظة تظهر مدبرة المنزل.

مدبرة المنزل
Sir, there's a lady at the door.
(موسيو ويليام، في مدام عالباب)

تظهر صوفيا خلفها.

مدبرة المنزل
Maam! (مدام!)

ويليام
It's ok (ماشي الحال)

تغادر مدبرة المنزل. ويليام يعدّل جلسته.صوفيا متجمّدة من وقع الصدمة، تبدو مذهولة لرؤيته في مثل هذه الحالة السيئة.

يدعوها للجلوس، فتجلس بقربه. يخيّم على اللحظة صمتٌ ثقيل.

ويليام

ممازحاً.

مأخرة، متل العادة.

صوفيا ترسم على وجهها ابتسامة خفيفة، بينما لا تزال تتأمّل حالته المزرية.

صوفيا
ليه عملت هيك؟

ويليام
صراحة قد ما عامل إشيا، مش أكيد عن شو عم تحكي بالزبط.

صوفيا
اختفيت وسكّرت خطّك وما عرفت شي عنّك.

ويليام
لمَا تطلّعي فيي مثل ما عم تطلّعي فيي هلّق.

صوفيا المتأثرة تشيح بنظرها عنه.

صوفيا
بعتذر، مش عم أعرف شو أعمل.
كتير معصّبة منك وبنفس الوقت ما عم أقدر...

صوفيا على وشك أن تجهش بالبكاء، يبدأ صوتها بخيانتها، فتصمت. ويليام يضع يده على ذراعها بلطف.

ويليام
هاي... أنا ماشي حالي.

صوفيا تنظر إليه من جديد.

صوفيا
واضح.

ويليام
ما تنغشّي بالمظاهر. أوقات المرض بيشفينا من كتير إشيا....
انتي كيفك؟

صوفيا
مش طايقتك

تبتسم

ويليام
بعرف... الحب إلو كذا وجّ أصلاً.

عندما تسمع إجابته، تهز رأسها وكأنها تقول: «هو نفسه ويليام القديم، لا يتغيّر».

ويليام
...في حدا بحياتك هالإيام؟ إذا لأ، عندي شب غير شكل لإلك. أوقات فيه يكون مزعج، كتير أوقات.

يضحك

بس شب كتير منيح، بينحب.

صوفيا تبتسم له، وتهّز رأسها مؤكدة حبّها لجاك.

صوفيا
مش قادرة شوفك هيك!

ويليام
لو ما صرلي هيك، يمكن ما كنتو رجعتوا إنت وجاك لبعضكن.

صوفيا تصفن فيه للحظات، ثم تقترب منه وتعانقه مطوّلاً.

المشهد ٥٥
حانة، ليلاً

جاك يدخل إلى أحد البيانو بار ثملاً ويتجه نحو الساقي.

الساقي
شو عبالك تشرب؟

جاك
عندك لبن؟

هاتف جاك يرنّ. إنها صوفيا، يضع الهاتف على الوضع الصامت. ينظر من حوله ويرى عازف بيانو يعزف على بيانو كبير.

Cut to

جاك مستلقياً تحت البيانو الكبير، بينما يستمر عازف البيانو في العزف. جاك يغمض عينيه ويسرح في ذكرياته مع صوفيا: صوفيا تستمع إلى إحدى أغنياتها المفضلة، تتفاعل معها وترقص على إيقاعها. جاك يشاهد مباراة كرة قدم، تدخل صوفيا ممازحة وتقف بينه وبين التلفزيون فاتحة ذراعيها لكي تحجب رؤيته.

صوفيا تطبخ، وفجأة تشتعل النيران في المقلاة.
صوفيا وجاك يتشاجران، تبدأ بالبكاء فيقترب منها ويحضنها.

جاك يفتح عينيه وهو لا يزال ممدداً تحت البيانو.

المشهد ٥٦
غرفة نوم ويليام، ليلاً

ويليام نائماً في سريره يشعر بحضورٍ ما في الغرفة.

ويليام
ماتيو؟

يظهر من خلف الجدار ثوب داكن فضفاض يصل إلى الأرض، مع قلنوسة واسعة تغطّي الرأس، مثل الثوب الذي يرتديه الكاهن الفرنسيسكاني.
ويليام لا يستطيع أن يميّز أحداً في داخله، وكأن الثوب فارغ.

ويليام
إنت مين؟!...شو بدّك مني؟!

الرداء المقنّع
إنتَ عم تناديلي.

تمرُّ ثوان قبل أن يستوعب خلالها ويليام أنه في حضرة ملاك الموت!

ويليام
ليش أنا؟!

الرداء المقنّع
وليش لأ؟ ولاّ حاسس إنه هالأرض ما بتبرم بلاك؟

ويليام
حاسس إنك ظالم. بكّير عليي!

الرداء المقنّع
هه! بتفتكروا إنو عندكن وقت. أنا الوقت!

ويليام يصمت. يبدأ الرداء المقنّع بالتراجع والانسحاب.

ويليام
ما تفلّ!

الرداء المقنّع
شو بعد بدّك؟

ويليام
ما بعرف.

الرداء المقنّع
ويليام العظيم خايف!

ويليام
وبعدين شو؟

الرداء المقنّع يختفي من الغرفة.

هاي! لوين آخدني؟!

المشهد ٥٧
منزل جاك وصوفيا

صوفيا نائمة في السرير. ينفتح باب المنزل ثم يغلق.

جاك يدخل الغرفة فيرى صوفيا نائمة. يتأمّلها للحظة، ثم يستلقي خلفها بكامل ملابسه ويحتضنها.

المشهد ٥٨
منزل ويليام

ويليام على سطيحة منزله مستلقياً على أريكته المفضلة وفي أذنيه سمّاعات. نراه غارقاً في أفكاره.
ماتيو يتشمّس بينما يتصفّح إحدى المجلات.

ويليام
بتعملّي فنجان قهوة؟

ماتيو
أكيد.

ماتيو يدخل إلى المنزل.

* موسيقى* “Channels and Winds” من تأليف فيليب غلاس و رافي شنكار تسمع في الخلفية

ويليام يبقى على أريكته متأملاً.لحظات تمرّ قبل أن ينهض ويتجّه ببطء نحو حوض السباحة. عندما يصل الى حافته، يلقي بنفسه في الماء.

تحت الماء، يرى نفس السيدتين ،أمه وأخته، في الطرف الآخر من الحوض، تبتسمان له. يحدّق فيهما قليلاً ثم يسبح نحوهما.

يعود ماتيو ومعه القهوة ولكنه لا يجد ويليام على الأريكة، يتفاجأ. ينظر حوله، ينصعق عند رؤية جسد ويليام في المسبح يطفو على سطح المياه، وجهه إلى الأسفل.

ماتيو

Non, non!

(لأ،لأ!)

ماتيو يقفز في الماء، ويسبح باتجاه ويليام، يمسك برأسه ويرفعه خارج المياه.

بليز لأ، بليز لأ!

المشهد ٥٩

في المستشفى

جاك يصعد درج المستشفى بخطى واسعة وسريعة.
ماتيو في قاعة الانتظار يجلس باكياً.
جاك يتجه مباشرة نحو العناية الفائقة ويدخل بدون إذن. تتبعه الممرضة معترضة على دخوله.

الممرّضة

جاك ما فيك تفوت...

جاك لا يُبالي بما تقوله ويتابع سيره.

الممرّضة

جاك عمول معروف!!!

حالة ويليام حرجة جدّاً. الدكتور فؤاد يجلس إلى جانبه ويمسك بيده.

جاك

كيفه؟

د. فؤاد يهزّ رأسه بيأسٍ وارتباك. تدخل إحدى الممرّضات.

الممرّضة

دكتور عاوزينك، في حالة طارئة.

د. فؤاد

شوفوا غيري.

الممرّضة

ما في حدا، دكتور سيمون فلّ.

دوكتور فؤاد يرافق الممرضة على مضض. جاك يقترب من ويليام ويجلس إلى جانبه. يمسك يده وينظر إليه، عاجزاً عن التفوّه بكلمة.

ويليام

يفتح عينيه بجهدٍ ويهمس.

إيلا ري.

جاك يبتسم رغماً عنه. ويليام يشعر بألمٍ شديد.
جاك يُداعب بيده جبين ويليام، وبيده الثانية يُمسك يد ويليام، ويهمس في أذنه.

جاك
منّك وحدك. منّك وحدك....

ويليام يتألم، جاك لا يزال يتكلّم معه همساً.

جاك
إنتَ بالجنينة عالمرجوحة وميوتشا حدّك.
وقعتوا عالأرض وعم تضحكوا...

Flashback

المشهد ٦٠
منزل ميوتشا القروي، نهاراً

ميوتشا تغرس يدها في شعر ويليام بعد سقوطهما من الأرجوحة الشبكية على الأرض في حديقة منزلها القروي لحظة التقاط الصورة.

Cut to

في العناية الفائقة، جاك لا يزال بجانب ويليام يتكلّم معه همساً.
عينا ويليام مفتوحتان كما لو أنه يرى النفق الأبيض.

Cut back

على الأرض، ويليام يعانق ميوتشا من الخلف، يشم رقبتها ويقبلها، بينما تمدُ ميوتشا ذراعيها خلفها لتلتفّ حول خصره، ممسكة بقميصه بكلتا يديها.
ويليام يفتح أزرار قميص ميوتشا الأبيض الواسع.

Cut back

في العناية، عينا ويليام مفتوحتان ولكن خاليتان من الحياة.
جاك ينظر إليه، وعيناه مغرورقتان بالدموع.

المشهد ٦١
مركز علاج السرطان، بعد أسبوع

جاك ينتظر في مكتب د. عمر. سكرتيرة الوزير تعمل على الكمبيوتر.

جاك
عفواً مدام، عندك فكرة ليش طالبني معاليه؟

السكرتيرة تهز رأسها نفياً.
يرن هاتف المكتب. السكرتيرة تجيب ثم تُنهي المكالمة.

السكرتيرة
تفضّل إذا بتريد، معاليه ناطرَك.

جاك
مرسي

الدكتور عمر جالساً خلف مكتبه، يُقلّب أوراقاً في أحد الملقّات.
جاك يدخل. ينهض د. عمر ليصافحه.

جاك
بونجور معاليك، طلبت تشوفني؟

د. عمر
نعم، تفضّل.

جاك يجلس أمامه.

د. عمر
ما شاء الله على هالملف، شهادات، دكتورا، وكل هالخبرة بعمرك!
بهنّيك.

جاك

يبدو متفاجئاً.

شكراً.

د. عمر
نحنا عم نفتّش على شخص يستلم قسم العلاج الفيزيائي،

وحابّين تكون إنت.

مذهولاً، يحاول جاك الكلام لكنه لا يقوى على ذلك.
أخيراً، يُصفّي حلقه ويستعيد صوته.

جاك
شرف إلي معاليك. أنا بشكرك.
س في إسأل كيف وصل ملفي لعندكم؟!

د. عمر
صديق مشترك.

جاك
صديق؟!

د. عمر
بتآمن بالملائكة؟

المشهد ٦٢
منزل ويليام

جاك والدكتور فؤاد يجلسان في الصالون قبالة بعضهما.

جاك
دخلك ما شفت ولا سمعت عن حدا من أهله.

د. فؤاد
والده توفّى هو وصغير. وخسر إمّه وإخته ورا بعضن.
كانوا نقطة ضعفه.

جاك
أوف!!!

يدخل ماتيو حاملاً علبة ويعطيها لجاك الذي ينظر إليه مستغرباً.

ماتيو
تركا ويليام مع إسمَك عليها.

يرن هاتف الدكتور فؤاد، فيبتعد إلى غرفة الجلوس.

Cut to

جاك يجلس على سرير ويليام ويحدّق في الصندوق الذي أعطاه إياه ماتيو. بعد لحظات، يفتحه. بداخله أسطوانة فينيل على غلافها صورة مغنية برازيلية، ميوتشا.

جاك
ميوتشا!

جاك مرتبك وحائر، يقلب الأسطوانة.

ينظر إلى العلبة مجدداً، ويرى في أسفلها صورة الأرجوحة الشبكية الفارغة التي استخدمها ويليام كعلامة مرجعية لكتابه.
جاك يقلب الصورة ويقرأ على ظهرها الكلمات التالية:

"To the best brother ever.
From Cyprus with love.
Miss you superstar"
Janine

(«من قبرص مع حبي.)
(إلى أفضل أخ في العالم.
) (اشتقتلّك يا سوبر ستار»)
(جانين)

جاك يخرج الأسطوانة من الغلاف ويشغّلها على القرص الدوار.
تصدح أغنية*«Voce vai ver» لمغنية برازيلية اسمها ميوتشا!

*

فيتذكر أنه سمعها من قبل في هذه الغرفة نفسها عندما كان يعالج ويليام، يوم قرر هذا الأخير سرد قصته.

جاك يخرج من الغرفة مسرعاً ويتجه نحو غرفة الجلوس حيث الدكتور فؤاد يتحدث مع ماتيو.

د. فؤاد
...خلّيك عم تهتمّ بالبيت لكنت رجعت أنا من السفر.

جاك يدخل كالمجنون.

جاك
دكتور فؤاد!

فؤاد يندهش من اندفاع جاك نحوه بهذه الطريقة.

جاك
بليز قلّي إنّك بتعرف ميوتشا!!

د. فؤاد
موتشي؟! مين موتشي؟!

جاك
ميوتشا، ميوتشا، المرا اللي كان يحبّا ويليام!

د. فؤاد
ما بحياتي سامع بهالإسم! في حدا إسمو ميوتشا؟!

جاك
إي! كان رح يتجوّزا ويليام بقبرص،
وفلّ آخر دقيقة! وإنت كنت الشبين!

د. فؤاد
أنا؟! شو كنت عم تتعاطى بالأوضة؟!
بعد فيه من أدوية ويليام؟!

جاك يسقط على الأريكة غارقاً في أفكاره، محاولاً استيعاب الحقيقة، وواقع أن ويليام كان ولايزال يتلاعب به حتى بعد وفاته.

المشهد ٦٣
قبر ويليام

صوفيا وقد بدت عليها علامات الحمل واضحة، برفقة جاك عند قبر ويليام.
تقترب وتضع باقة من الورود عند شاهد القبر.
تبقى مكانها للحظات متأملة مع امتنان واضح في عينيها،
ثم تلتفت نحو جاك.

صوفيا

تضع يدها على حملها.

أنا وويليام رح ننطرك بالسيارة.

صوفيا تداعب خد جاك برفق، بينما هو يضع يده بحنانٍ فوق يدها التي تغطي حملها.

صوفيا تغادر المقبرة.
جاك ينفخ الغبار عن حافة القبر، ثم يمسحها بيده ويجلس.

جاك

إيلا ري يا صاحبي، كيفك اليوم؟
من هلّق ورايِح رح نغيّر عادتنا، أنا اللي بحكي وإنت بتِسمع.

جاك يطلق ضحكة خفيفة لنفسه.

مبارِح كان عيد زواجنا الثالث.
في قِلَّك إنّو المفاجأة كانت شغلة كتير كبيرة.
حتّى إنت ما كنت فكّرت فيا.

جاك يبتسم مازحاً ومُتفاخراً.

مزبوط إنه التلميذ بيتفوّق عالإستاذ!!

جاك يضحك مجدداً.

بقدر إتخايل شو كنت رح تجاوبني لو كنت قادر تِحكي....
إشتقتلّك، إلو زمان ما حدا بهدلني.
كل ما بشوف كاسة لبن بضحك لوحدي متل المسطول.

يأخذ من جيبه بطحة كونياك وسيغاراً، يشعل السيغار.

جاك

أنا أكيد إنّك رح تشم ريحته.

رافعاً بطحة الكونياك.

كاسك يا صاحبي، اللي متلك ما بموتوا!

جاك يخرج من جيبه صورة الأرجوحة الشبكية الفارغة، ينظر إليها بتمعّن ويضعها على شاهد قبر ويليام نسيم خفيف يجعل أوراق الأشجار المتساقطة على الأرض تدور حول الصورة.

تُسمَع في الخلفية أغنية ميوتشا «Você vai ver».

zoom in على الصورة. عندما تكاد الصورة تملأ الإطار، تبدأ الأرجوحة الفارغة بالتمايل بخفّة مع النسيم الذي يحرّك أوراق الأشجار خارج الصورة، على صدى ضحكات ويليام وميوتشا.

Fade Out